LUKE'S PORTRAIT OF JESUS

LUKE'S

PORTRAIT OF

JESUS

HUGH MARTIN
D.D.

SCM PRESS LTD
56 Bloomsbury Street London WC1

First published March 1949

Distributed in Canada by our exclusive agents
The Macmillan Company of Canada Limited,
70 Bond Street, Toronto

Printed in Great Britain by
Northumberland Press Limited
Gateshead on Tyne

CONTENTS

TO THE READER

THE Gospel according to St. Luke has always meant more to me than any other single book in the New Testament or out of it. I have tried here to share with others something of what it has meant to me, and especially with those who have not the time or the training for following the work of the scholars. No professional student is likely to read this book, but if he does he will find, I hope, that I have taken due account of the researches of the experts. Its aim and scope ruled out its equipment with large numbers of footnotes giving references to authorities or indicating the nature of the controversies where experts disagree: but perhaps the scholar, reading between the lines, will see that I am not unaware of them. For the same reason, quotations have been reduced to a minimum, though I hope that any direct indebtedness has been acknowledged. Indirectly I am debtor to a host.

This is not a commentary, though most passages in the Gospel are discussed, often more than once from different angles. I have given numerous Biblical references in the hope that some will read this with the Bible beside them.

The best commentaries known to me on St. Luke's Gospel for the general reader are those by William Manson in the *Moffatt New Testament Commentaries,* and by Henry Balmforth in the *Clarendon Bible.*

TO THE READER

I

ST. LUKE AND HIS GOSPEL

Welcome, all wonders in one sight!
  Eternity shut in a span!
Summer in winter! day in night!
  Heaven in earth! and God in man!
Great little One, whose all-embracing birth,
Lifts earth to heaven, stoops heaven to earth.

Richard Crashaw

THE Christian message is inseparably concerned with Jesus of Nazareth, of Gethsemane, of Calvary, of the empty tomb. The German philosopher Lessing once urged that it was impossible to make the truth dependent upon the contingent events of history. To many people that seems sensible, even axiomatic. But the truth of Christianity does depend upon the historical facts that Jesus lived in a particular place at a particular time, that He died, that He rose again. That was what created Christianity. That was the burden of the first preaching—not 'the Fatherhood of God and the brotherhood of man'. The Hill of Calvary rather than the Mount of the Sermon stood out in the minds of the early Christians.

This is not true of all religions. Forget me if only you remember the teaching, said the Buddha. Judaism and Parseeism would not be seriously affected if it were proved that Moses and Zoroaster were merely legendary: the teaching would still remain. But there would be nothing left of Christianity if Jesus were shown to be a myth. When Paul had to put his message in a sentence he cried, 'Believe in the Lord Jesus Christ!' 'Jesus is Lord' was the first creed of the Church.

'That which we have seen and heard declare we unto you' (1 John 1.3). The revelation of God had been given through historic events. The Word had become flesh.

1

The first preaching centred in the story of the Cross and

the Resurrection, as may be seen from the early chapters of Acts. But the value of the crucifixion of course depended upon the one who hung on the Cross. The story must always have had a preface. Cavalry pointed back to Galilee (Acts 2.22; 10.38).

The earliest Christian writings that have come down to us are letters written by the Apostle Paul to the churches, mostly occasional in character and dealing with local problems. They take for granted the fact of Christ and knowledge of His life and teaching. (e.g. 1 Cor. 11.1,23-25; 9.5; 15.3ff.; 2 Cor. 5.21;8.9; 10.1; 1 Thess. 4.2; Gal. 4.4.) Contemporary with the epistles, oral instruction was being given in the Christian community and written records also began to take shape at quite an early date. First of all was probably the basic story of the Passion, but there were also collections of sayings of Jesus and stories about Him. Apparently also there was a collection of Old Testament passages which were thought to point to Jesus as the promised Messiah.

In those early days there could have been no lack of reminiscences of Jesus. Thousands who had seen Him and heard Him would be eager to add their stories to the common stock at the church meeting. (1 Cor. 14.26.) The trouble would be not to find stories but to sift them. The 'best' stories, the most typical, the most characteristic, the most helpful, would tend to survive.

One of the reasons for repeating the stories would be the desire to know what Jesus would wish them to do about their own problems—the observance of the Sabbath, or fasting, or marriage, or whatever it might be. The discussion of a problem would prompt the telling of a story. Someone would say: 'I remember on one occasion that the Lord Jesus said so and so, or did so and so.'

To recognize that the practical needs of the Christian life influenced the selection and preservation of some of the stories is not to say that the Church invented the stories to suit itself. Some of the modern 'form critics' have maintained this, but it is contrary to the evidence and to all the probabilities. The problems discussed in the Gospels are those of the contemporaries of Jesus, rather than those of the later Church. If the stories had been invented they would surely have been better adapted to the purpose, and we should not find so many urgent problems of the early Church left without appropriate stories. That some unconscious adaptation took place would be only natural, and the words of Jesus might sometimes be misunderstood. But no church meeting or group of church meetings could have invented such matchless pithy sayings as are attributed to Jesus. There are a few which raise questions in our mind because they do not seem to be in character, but the great majority have a self-authenticating note. 'I have no hesitation in saying,' writes Dr. Vincent Taylor,[1] 'that the tradition of the words of Jesus is far better preserved than we have any right to expect, and with much greater accuracy than is to be found in the records of the words of any great teacher of the past.'

More than utilitarian motives would be at work. One great motive would be simply the desire to know all they could about the Lord they loved. Memories must have been treasured for their own sake, and not only because they were useful to preachers as illustrations.

The first Christians were too busy preaching to devote energy to book production, and at first there seemed little need for books. There were many first-hand witnesses. Oral teaching and 'learning by heart' was the most natural method in an age when books were scarce and reading an unusual accomplishment. Even in Palestine with its synagogue schools, memories were practised and tenacious. Jewish Rabbis were accustomed to teach their disciples word by word till the lesson was memorized. Perhaps such a lesson is illustrated in the giving of the Lord's Prayer (11.1). A large proportion of the sayings of Jesus show the characteristic rhythms and parallelisms of Hebrew poetry. Perhaps He put a summary of His longer talks into such a form so that they might be readily remembered. Sometimes there seems careful preparation of the very words and shape of His teaching.[2] Some of the unforgettable sayings were perhaps, as Dr. E. F. Scott suggests, 'the hammer blows by which He finally drove home the truths He had been expounding'.[3]

[1] *The Formation of the Gospel Tradition*, p. 113.
[2] See e.g. 17.26-30; 12.24-48. On the general point see Burney, *The Poetry of Our Lord* and Moffatt's translation of the Gospels.
[3] *The Validity of the Gospel Record*, p. 127.

But as the years passed by and the Lord, contrary to expectation, did not return and the eye-witnesses began to die and the Church spread farther and farther from its Palestinian centre, the need for more permanent records became apparent. Different churches gathered together stories long familiar to them. 'It becomes increasingly likely . . . that much of the material which was later incorporated in the Gospels, was in written form at an earlier date than is commonly allowed. If we ask what literature the Church possessed at the time when Paul and Barnabas set out on the first Missionary Journey, the answer will be: the Old Testament; an outline of the Ministry of Jesus and a detailed account of the Passion, the latter in a fixed form if not written down; a collection of the teachings of Jesus (Q) probably in writing; possibly other collections of material—parables, conflict-stories, proof texts from the Old Testament, either written down or on the way to being written down.'[1] The Gospels, as we have them, are later than the epistles but they incorporate material which is earlier than the earliest epistle. The Gospel writers were not for the first time collecting anecdotes and sayings: they were putting together into more permanent form material already in circulation.

2

Among the 'Gospels'[2] that gradually took shape, four won for themselves a pre-eminent place; because of their comparative fulness, or authoritativeness, or because they recorded the tradition as it had come down to the leading churches, of Rome, Antioch, Ephesus, or Caesarea. One of the four was 'the Gospel according to St. Luke'. Its preface makes clear that there were earlier written documents, based in their turn upon an oral tradition going back to the first eye-witnesses. Here is a paraphrase of it in modern speech: 'The attempt has been made in many quarters to draw up a narrative of those facts, the occurrence and results of which have led to the existence of our society, namely the Church, whose belief is founded on the

---

[1] T. W. Manson, *A Companion to the Bible,* p. 99.
[2] The word Gospel, originally ' good spell ' or good tidings, first meant the contents of the books and was later applied to the books themselves.

traditions of persons who from the beginning were eye-witnesses and ministers of the word. I have determined to take a further step. I have once more traced the course of the whole series of events with accurate research, and I now present you, most excellent Theophilus, with an ordered history, that you may by means of this fuller treatment be reassured as to the accuracy of those points on which you have already received summary information.'[1]

Luke tells us that there were ' many ' accounts of the life of Jesus in existence. He made use of these and, in addition, went where he could to original sources; doing in fact what any competent modern historian seeks to do. Study shows that there are peculiarly close relations between the first three Gospels, which overlap, agree and diverge in the most surprising and intricate ways. Compared with the Fourth Gospel they possess a similar ground plan and a similar approach to their subject. Hence they have been called ' the Synoptic Gospels '.

Like Matthew, Luke had before him Mark's Gospel and incorporated about half of it almost word for word in his own. Modern ideas of copyright did not then exist and quotation marks had not been invented. Neither Mark as author nor his readers would feel any sense of proprietorship in this record of the tradition of the Christian community. From the amount of common matter in Matthew and Luke, in addition to their quotations from Mark, it is necessary to presume the existence of another document which they both used. This is known to scholars as Q, from the German word *Quelle,* meaning source. It was apparently composed almost entirely of sayings, with little narrative, and may have been the collection of ' oracles ' which Papias says that the Apostle Matthew collected. In any case it was probably originally compiled in Aramaic, the language of Jesus, and translated into Greek before the middle of the first century. As a third source Luke had a considerable amount of material of his own, of which more will be said later.

None of the Gospels provides us with a ' biography ' of Jesus, in the modern sense. We do not know what He looked like. Very little is said about His childhood and education. Even of the three years or so of His active

[1] S. C. Carpenter, *Christianity According to St. Luke,* p. 148.

ministry the greater part is unrecorded. All that has been preserved out of the mass of reminiscences current in the early Church is a comparatively small number of typical stories and sayings. Many of the stories survived with no record of their original setting and they have apparently been inserted into the framework at what seemed appropriate points.

Some scholars have even maintained that the early Church was not at all interested in the sequence of events in the life of Jesus, apart from the story of Passion Week. But that is going too far. In Mark's Gospel we do have the outlines of a life and not simply an impression of a character: there is movement and shape in the narrative. Yet even Mark starts his story when Jesus was already about thirty years of age, though he does not tell us so.

Luke's Gospel is the nearest approach to a 'life' with biographical interest, and he attempts to relate his story to contemporary events. But even he is not a historian in the modern sense. He is rather the custodian of a message. His avowed object is to prove to Theophilus that the Faith he has accepted has sound historical foundations. Luke was certainly concerned to be accurate. The details of his Gospel and of the Acts have proved to be remarkably reliable. Again and again statements of his that had been much criticized and suspected, have been proved by research and discovery to be accurate. Some few that are still under fire may yet receive similar vindication.

Some critics appear to start from the assumption that the Gospel story is largely fictitious and that whatever happened it was not that. They wax scornful of attempts to reconcile apparently inconsistent accounts in the Synoptics but will produce much more improbable and complicated theories of their own to show how the 'original' story became changed into what we now have. We need not contend that there are no errors of fact in the Gospel story or that the record has not at times been coloured in the telling by the experience of the Christian community. But we can maintain that the writers had an honest desire to be accurate. We can credit the early Church with as much concern to distinguish between what Jesus said and did not say as any modern student. Note, for example, the care with which St. Paul distinguishes between what he believes to be the teaching of the Lord and his own opinion. (1 Cor. 7.10,12,25,40.) Such a sense of responsibility in so sacred a matter as the words of their Lord can surely be expected in the New Testament writers generally.

Luke is interpreter, as well as historian. He has a thesis to put forward. But that thesis grew for him out of the facts: he is not inventing facts to fit the thesis. If a modern historian claims that he is completely unbiased and has formed no judgment or point of view about his period, his claim is very unlikely to be true. Nor does it follow that if it were true he would be a better historian. It is possible to interpret without distorting the facts. For Luke the Gospel was in the historical facts themselves. It was bound up with the reality of the life and teaching of Jesus. This is no 'once upon a time' story.

Not only the inherent probability of the case but the results of generations of the most meticulous examination of the documents, justify us in believing in the substantial accuracy of the Gospel record. 'The more critical our study has been,' writes Professor C. H. Dodd, 'the more sure we become that here is a real Person in history, many-sided, often perplexing, certainly too great to be reduced to any common type, and not fully intelligible to us; but for all that unmistakably individual, strongly defined in lines of character and purpose, and challenging us all by a unique outlook on life. Browning is right,

> That one Face, far from vanish, rather grows,
> Or decomposes but to recompose.

After the discipline of historical criticism we do know Jesus better and whatever was faulty in the traditional Christianity that has come down to us, or in our apprehension of it, is confronted afresh with the Reality that started it all.'[1]

It is in that belief that we embark upon this examination of 'Luke's Portrait of Jesus'.

3

We have so far been taking for granted the traditional ascription of the third of our Gospels to St. Luke. At this

[1] *The Authority of the Bible*, pp. 230f.

point it is proper to inquire ' who was Luke, and did he in fact write the Gospel? '

The Gospel and the Acts of the Apostles claim in their prefaces to be written by the same hand, and there is every reason to accept this. From the middle of the second century references in surviving literature declare that this writer was Luke, the Greek doctor and companion of the Apostle Paul. The tendency in cases of doubt was to ascribe authorship to outstanding leaders of the Church, and Luke was hardly in that class. There is therefore good reason for accepting this verdict of tradition.

The New Testament names Luke three times. Paul tells us (Col. 4.14) that ' Luke, the beloved physician,' was with him in his imprisonment. The Letter to Philemon (verse 24) names him as a fellow labourer. The courageous but pathetic close of the Second Letter to Timothy says ' Only Luke is with me ' (2 Tim. 4.11). He is loyal to his friend to the last. Irenaeus in the second century spoke of Luke as ' inseparable from Paul '. It is an attractive guess that he may be the ' true yoke-fellow ' of Philippians 4.3; especially in view of his close connection with the church at Philippi and the fact that he is not mentioned in the epistle as being then with Paul.

There are passages in Acts where the author takes to speaking in the first person as having been himself present, using ' we ' instead of ' they '. No other known companion of St. Paul could have been present on all these occasions.

It has been suggested that he may be Lucius of Cyrene, who was an elder at Antioch (Acts 13.1). One reading of Acts 11.27 (in the ' Western ' text) reads ' And in those days came prophets from Jerusalem to Antioch and there was much gladness, and when *we* were collected together, one of them named Agabus,' etc. If this reading is accepted it further connects Luke with Antioch: it makes him a member of the Christian congregation at Antioch to which Agabus prophesied the famine of A.D. 46. Eusebius definitely asserts that he was born there. This Syrian city is described by Josephus as the most important in the Empire after Rome and Alexandria. It was a cosmopolitan spot, a meeting place of East and West, one of the cradles of the Christian Church, and the birthplace of the name ' Christian ' (Acts 11.26).

It has also been suggested that he was the 'man of Macedonia' whom Paul saw in his dream (Acts 16.9). Verse 10 shows that Luke was then with Paul. Luke apparently took an active share in the evangelistic work at Philippi (16.13-17). The evidence of the 'we' passages suggests that he was left behind there, perhaps in charge of the church, until Paul returned six years later (Acts 20.5).

Perhaps they first met when Luke was called in as a medical adviser. We know that Paul had a great deal of illness. It is certain at least that Luke was a doctor, and there has been much discussion among scholars as to the 'medical language' used in the Gospel. Many of these 'medical' words were in fact used by a number of contemporary writers who were not doctors, which suggests that they belonged to the vocabulary of any educated man. But their presence is at least consistent with the writer being a doctor and taken with other evidence of his keen interest in disease and healing confirm the case for attributing the work to 'Dr. Luke'. The revision of Mark's account of the healing of the woman with the issue of blood suggests concern for the credit of the profession (cf. Mark 5.26 and Luke 8.43).

Certainly the cumulative force of the evidence confirms the traditional ascription of the Third Gospel to Luke. Even when all that is merely conjecture is laid aside, we know a good deal about him. In many old paintings the artist has included a self-portrait of himself among the crowd, perhaps as one of a little group kneeling before the Cross. Luke was not concerned to talk about himself. His gaze was fixed upon his Lord. But none the less his own portrait is there in the background. He reveals himself in the way he tells his story.

4

The native language of Jesus was Aramaic. The Gospels however are written in Greek, the common language of the civilized world, even though Rome was its ruler. Years ago, however, scholars realized that the Greek of the New Testament was not the classical Greek of Plato or Demosthenes. It was sometimes described as 'the language of the Holy Ghost'. Modern discoveries in the sands of Egypt have revealed in a fascinating way that in fact the Holy Ghost spoke in the language of the common people of the day. There was in popular use a more colloquial dialect, the *koine* or 'common' Greek, and it was in this that the New Testament was written.

But the Aramaic background ought not to be forgotten. Modern study of this has enabled scholars to throw much light on the Gospels. Some of the differences between Matthew and Luke may be due to different renderings of an Aramaic original. For example, at one point it looks as if Luke (11.41) had confused two similar Aramaic words, *dakki*, 'cleanse' and *zakki*, 'give alms'. Matthew's reading of 'cleanse' (23.26) is more intelligible.

5

Luke's special investigations are reflected in the fact that a large proportion of his Gospel is found only there, including some of the best loved stories in the New Testament; such as some of the nativity stories and the parables of the Good Samaritan, the Prodigal Son, the Lost Sheep, the Lost Coin, the Pharisee and the Publican, the Rich Fool, Dives and Lazarus, and the Friend at midnight. Luke must have been the recipient of many reminiscences of Jesus. We can see that he had special opportunities for securing information from people with first-hand knowledge. Apparently he spent several years at Caesarea during Paul's imprisonment. There he met Mnason 'an early disciple' (Acts 21.16), and stayed with Philip and his daughters (Acts 21.8ff.). From Caesarea he could easily visit Galilee and Jerusalem (cf. Acts 21.15ff.). He met the Apostle James. It is possible that the Virgin Mary was still alive, perhaps living with James in Jerusalem. It has often been suggested that some of Luke's nativity stories must come ultimately, and may have come directly, from her. They are certainly told from a woman's point of view. Luke seems also to have had special information about Herod's court, perhaps through Joanna (8.3) or Manaen (Acts 13.1).

6

Opinions are sharply divided as to the date of the Gospel.

The argument largely turns upon one's judgment as to whether the references to the siege of Jerusalem, especially when compared with the vaguer statements in Mark 13, prove that Luke was writing after the event in A.D. 70. He reports Jesus (19.43) as saying that the enemies would surround Jerusalem and dig a trench about her. But this is an obvious way of describing any siege, and is almost a quotation from Isaiah 29.3 or Ezekiel 4.2. In chapter 21.20-24 there is a more detailed description. But if Luke is modifying original words of Jesus to make them fit the event, as is alleged, why does he leave unaltered the advice to flee · to the mountains, since in fact the Christians fled to Pella in the Jordan valley? There is no reason why Jesus should not have foreseen the siege and fall of Jerusalem, without ascribing to Him any supernatural knowledge. Savonarola gave a detailed forecast in 1496 of the fall of Rome which took place in 1527. There is no necessity on this ground to insist upon a date after A.D. 70.

Another factor is the date of Acts, which was written after the Gospel (see Acts 1.1). Acts ends with Paul in Rome awaiting trial. If it was written after his martyrdom surely Luke would have mentioned the fact of his death, which probably took place in A.D. 64. This argument points to A.D. 60 to 63 as the date for the Gospel. To this it has been replied that perhaps Luke intended to write a third volume, and that he leaves Paul established in Rome, the capital of the empire, as a dramatic climax to Volume Two.

The balance of evidence seems to point to the earlier date, but it must be remembered that many scholars think otherwise. Even if the later date be accepted the Gospel was still published in the lifetime of people who had known Jesus.

7

The dedication to Theophilus, a Roman official, does not of course mean that Luke was writing for him alone. He had in view not only the Christian community, but probably also outsiders whose sympathy might be secured. Both Gospel and Acts contain many suggestions that they may be meant as an apologia for Christianity to the empire. Not only does Luke explain the unfamiliar Palestinian setting, but he is concerned to make it clear that Jesus was no political agitator and was unjustly condemned. He emphasizes the friendly relations of Paul with the Roman authorities.

8

Luke was a writer of consummate skill. Merely as a piece of literature, his Gospel is one of the treasures of the world. In an often quoted phrase Renan called it ' the most beautiful book we possess '. Luke writes with more attention to literary style than the other evangelists. Some of his revisions of Mark seem to have the improvement of the Greek as their motive. The only Greek by birth among the New Testament writers, he complies with the literary conventions of his time in the carefully framed Preface, which shows a number of interesting affinities with similar prefaces in medical treatises by Hippocrates, Galen and others. The rest of his first two chapters breathes a different atmosphere, the setting of simple devoted lives in Palestinian Judaism; Hebraic not Greek. He can sketch a character in a few vivid words. He was no scissors and paste editor but has woven his varied material into a unity. An illustration of his skill is seen in setting the visit of Jesus to the synagogue at Nazareth right in the forefront of His ministry (though, as he makes clear, it came later in time) because it strikes the keynote to all that follows.

The legend that Luke was a painter cannot be traced farther back than the sixth century, but there seems no motive for inventing it and it may perhaps be true. Certainly he has the painter's eye for colour and grouping, and his Gospel has been the cause of many paintings.

> Give honour unto Luke evangelist,
> For it was he, the ancient legends say,
> Who first taught Art to fold her hands and pray.

To these words of Rossetti we may add Keble's:

> Taught by thee the church prolongs
> Her hymns of high thanksgiving still.

For the first chapters contain canticles which Christendom will never let die.

Luke's purpose is to paint a true portrait of ' the Lord Jesus'. He is not repeating all the stories he knows, nor is he concerned merely to satisfy biographical curiosity. The stories he chooses from the tradition of the Church are those he believes to be both reliable and representative. He seems frequently to record one story as typical of many incidents of the same kind. The Sermon at Nazareth (4.16-30) is representative of Jesus in the synagogue. There are typical healing miracles. He shows Jesus in the homes of his friends when he tells of the home in Bethany. When Jesus visits Zacchaeus, Luke wishes us to see Him seeking the outcast. When He stands by the bier in Nain, He is present at every death-bed. We are meant to see these stories cumulatively building up a portrait.

It is said that when Bernini, the Roman sculptor, was commissioned to make a statue of Charles the First, Vandyck drew three portraits for him on one canvas. One drawing showed the king's head turned to the right, another to the left, and the third was full face. Our Gospels show Jesus from different standpoints. No one Gospel can exhaust the subject. But to many the portrait of Luke is the most attractive of all and emphasizes aspects of the personality of Jesus that most capture their allegiance. In this book we are trying to look at Jesus through the eyes of St. Luke and from his standpoint.

' These most sacred writings,' said Erasmus of the Gospels, ' bring back to you a living image of His mind, the very Christ speaking, healing, dying, rising, in fact so wholly present that you would see less of Him if you beheld Him before your eyes.'

II

THE CHILD JESUS

See then the boy in first encounter with beauty,
his nativ wonder awaken'd by the motion of love;
as when live air, breathing upon a smother'd fire,
shooteth the smouldering core with tiny flames—so he
kindleth at heart with eternal expectancies
and the dream within him looketh out at his eyes.
        The Testament of Beauty (iv. 39ff.), Robert Bridges

THE Preface to Luke's Gospel belongs in manner and language to the cultured world of Greek literature. Then at once, in the remainder of the first two chapters (1.5-2.52), he transports us to the simple old-fashioned setting of a group of devout Jewish peasants, and his language changes in sympathy, taking on the colour of the Greek Old Testament. It is somewhat as if a modern writer after a polished and very up-to-date introduction wrote his first chapter in the English of the Authorized Version as he described some scene of seventeenth-century life.

There seems little doubt that Luke is making use of an earlier document, or documents, in Hebrew or Aramaic, coming from the Palestine of the stories themselves. Scholars are divided as to the extent of his own handiwork in this section; whether he is translating the work of others or himself giving a skilful and appropriate framework for material he has collected. In either event he shows his sympathy and artistic mastery. Luke was a Gentile and he saw Christianity as a universal faith, but he knew that ' salvation is of the Jews ' (John 4.22). His Gospel has the Jewish setting of the events it records, and nowhere more so than in these lovely chapters with their sympathetic picture of Jewish home life and religion. Writing for Gentile readers he is not so concerned as the first Gospel to discuss the teaching of Jesus about the old Law or to emphasize every link with the Old Testament. He is at pains to explain Jewish terms and practices. Yet he knows he is telling the story of a Divine process of revelation that began long years before, that culminated in Jesus, and, as he planned to tell in his second volume, that was destined to carry its message of God's love to all nations (24.47). He writes as an active member of an expanding Church. But it all began in Bethlehem, Nazareth, and Jerusalem. The Jewish people, said Athanasius, were ' the sacred school of the knowledge of God for all mankind '.

1

The Judaism of the time of Jesus had many aspects. In the group who welcomed Him, Zacharias, the priest, and his wife Elizabeth, Simeon and Anna, Mary and Joseph, are representative of its finest flowering. Simeon may stand for them all; a man both ' just and devout ' (2.25), that is, a good neighbour to his fellow men and a humble servant and worshipper of God. Men felt that he lived in the divine presence and that ' the Holy spirit was upon him '. Among the Pharisees were many fine personalities, but as a class they had made the Law which should have been written in their hearts into an external affair of regulations and observances. In their anxiety to be broad-minded and in touch with modern thought, the Sadducees had created a secularized humanism. There were fiery nationalists who could see nothing in Judaism but a programme of political freedom and revenge. But there were Simeons too who had kept true religion alive, and hearts open to receive the Christ when in God's good time He should come.

The vivid picture of this expectant religious group is so true to the spiritual situation of Judaism before Christ as the research of scholars has revealed it, and is so free from anachronisms, that it would be next to impossible for a Gentile writing sixty years later to invent it. The canticles carry their own evidence of contemporary origin.

These canticles, of course, are poetry, some of the best-known and treasured poetry of Christendom. But it is noteworthy that much in these chapters beside the accepted canticles, the Magnificat and the Benedictus and the Nunc

Dimittis, is poetry too. There are six other passages with all the characteristics of Hebrew verse; the words of Gabriel to Zacharias (1.13-17) and to Mary (1.30-33; 35-37), Elizabeth's greeting (1.42-45), the angel's message to the shepherds (2.10-12) and the words of Simeon to Mary (2.34-35). ' The Birth Stories,' writes Dr. Vincent Taylor,[1] ' represent the Evangelist's attempt, with the material at his disposal, to express in a poetic and imaginative form definite convictions about the birth and divine significance of Jesus.' We have here, says H. K. Luce, ' the imaginative poetry of devotion rather than the sober prose of history '. To recognize this will save us from misunderstanding and from the thankless attempt to rationalize every detail. Which is quite another thing from saying that the stories were invented. The writer of the preface could never have gone on immediately to record fables.

Is it not likely, for example, that the appearances of Gabriel were to the inner eye, not materializations in physical form, and that the words are an attempt to give fitting expression to an inner message? While it would be wrong to assert dogmatically that the canticles could not have been the spontaneous creation of moments of intense experience, it is at least possible that in their present polished form with their many reminiscences of the Old Testament they represent very early Christian hymns appropriately expressing the occasion. We cannot always distinguish in these stories between the historical kernel and the poetic setting.

2

Many good Christians have found difficulty in accepting the story of the Virgin Birth. I hope to show good cause why I for one accept it, but I am quite sure that the Virgin Birth is not a necessary, fundamental part of the Christian Faith, and that Christians who indulge in heresy hunts on this score are wrong. Our belief that Jesus is the Son of God is not based upon any conviction regarding the nature of His physical conception. It is a spiritual judgment on spiritual grounds. Further it is an undoubted fact that the

[1] *Op. cit.*, p. 161.

Virgin Birth was not part of the central Christian message as proclaimed by the apostles. The Virgin Birth is asserted in two Gospels only, Matthew and Luke. The remainder of the New Testament is silent, though it contains nothing inconsistent with the belief, and there are a few verses that have been thought to hint at it. (Gal. 4.4; Rom. 1.3; 5.12-21; 1 Cor. 15.44-49.) Possibly the truth was known to the apostles but kept secret during Mary's lifetime. In any case, it is not inevitably bound up with the heart of the Christian Gospel, and there are sincere Christians who find the belief more of a hindrance than a help. But there are also many who, believing on quite other grounds in the divinity of Christ, find the Virgin Birth a fitting accompaniment of His divinity. *Talis partus decet Deum*, wrote St. Ambrose: ' Such a birth was fitting for God.' The story is unique, but so is Jesus.

In the nature of the case the historical evidence must be limited, and the story if true must ultimately rest upon its having been made known by our Lord's Mother. One thing is clear, Matthew and Luke believe it to be a soundly attested fact. It is also clear from the differences of their accounts that they rely upon different streams of tradition, or in other words secured the evidence that convinced them from two different sources. There is no reason for doubting that the relevant verses (1.34-35) of St. Luke's Gospel were part of the original text. Attempts to remove them are based upon the desire to be rid of them, not upon grounds of textual evidence.

It is asserted by some that the story is an invention. But, one may ask, who invented it, and why?

There was no expectation among the Jews that the Messiah would be born of a virgin. The often quoted verse from Isaiah (7.14) was never so interpreted by Jews, and the word translated ' virgin' simply means ' young woman'. The high regard of the Jews for home and family would not encourage any such belief.

It is sometimes said that there are many pagan parallels to the story and that it is copied from them. There are certainly many pagan stories of superhuman births, but they are as different as could be from the Gospel narrative. In any case this is a Jewish story through and through. Nothing can be more certain than that this story does not come from a pagan source. And indeed nothing would horrify any devout Jew more than copying a pagan story of such a kind.

Can it then be a case of Christians at a later date garnishing the Gospel with legends intended to heighten the story? Again we must point out that this story comes from a Jewish background, and a pre-Christian Jewish background too. Nearly all scholars are agreed that the documents behind it embody the oldest material in the New Testament. This is not a later invention. Fortunately, perhaps, from this point of view, we are in no doubt as to what the legend makers in fact did when they got to work. There are quite a number of such documents conveniently grouped together in *The Apocryphal New Testament,* by M. R. James. In a section devoted to ' Infancy Gospels ' there is an amazing collection of fantastic and often unworthy stories about the birth and childhood of both Mary and Jesus. For example, Jesus at the age of five makes sparrows out of clay which come to life and fly away when he claps his hands. A child who bumps into Jesus is rebuked and dies. When the pitcher is broken Jesus brings water home in his cloak. And so on *ad nauseam.* It is all in most revealing contrast to the reserve, simplicity and sobriety of the Gospels.

Here then is the story of the Virgin Birth. It clearly comes from a Jewish source—yet there was no Jewish expectation that the Messiah would be born supernaturally. The story is certainly no copy of any imaginary pagan parallel. It is not in the least like the work of a later legend monger, and indeed bears upon the face of it the marks of an early origin. Who, I ask again, would invent such a story and why? And if, on other grounds, one believes that in Jesus the Word of God became flesh, the unique and supreme moment in human history, it is not hard to believe also that God in His wisdom chose a unique method for a unique event.

The facts would be known at first only within the family, and in part to the Mother only. It would be only to the most intimate confidants that her secret would be made known. There is much to suggest the voice of the Mother behind the story, and it has often been suggested that she may have told it herself to the doctor's ear. Another suggestion is that it might have come through Joanna, whom Luke mentions four times in his Gospel, and who was a close companion of Mary. But we have of course no real knowledge as to the method of transmission.

3

The Census recorded by Luke as happening at the time of the birth of Jesus was for long the ground for vigorous attacks on the reliability of the whole story. It was known that Quirinius was governor in Syria in A.D. 6, and that a census was taken then which led to a riot (Acts 5.37. Josephus *Antiquities*, 18.1.1). It was alleged that Luke had transferred all this to 8-6 B.C., the probable date of Jesus' birth. Until quite recent times there was no evidence, apart from Luke's statement, that there was any census at the proper time and there was definite evidence that someone else was then governor.

It would be too much to say that all the difficulties have been removed, but up to a point at least, Luke's accuracy has been corroborated in the most extraordinary fashion by the researches of W. M. Ramsay and others. We now know that there were enrolments every fourteen years in Egypt; there is papyrus evidence for A.D. 90, 48 and 20. Tacitus refers to one in A.D. 34. If the series be carried on one would have fallen at the right time. An Egyptian edict regarding the enrolment of A.D. 104 contains instructions for householders to return to their homes for the purpose. And evidence was found on two inscriptions at Antioch that Quirinius was in an official position in Syria, from B.C. 11-8. This is probably the reason why Luke says (2.2. R.V.) that this was the *first* enrolment that took place under Quirinius. Luke's reliability has been proved in similar dramatic fashion in relation to many of his statements in Acts. He has every claim to be treated with respect as a historian even where other corroborating evidence is lacking.

4

In the story of Simeon's welcome to the infant Jesus the universal character of the Gospel is already proclaimed (2.22-35). How did Simeon recognize Jesus? A peasant woman with her baby was a common enough sight. We do not know. We can only imagine some gift of spiritual discernment that sensed what was hidden from others. Simeon was looking and waiting for God, expecting Him to act, and it is to the listening and expectant heart that God reveals Himself. He had an overwhelming conviction that he would not die till he saw the Messiah: till then he must keep his watch.

In this baby he hailed the response to the age-long expectations of his people, the consolation of Israel, the hope of the nations. And like a tired sentry after a long spell of night duty he thanks God for his relief in a moving poem. It is the word for the relief of a sentry that he uses: 'Now Lord, thou art dismissing thy servant.' It is a statement of fact, not a petition. So at the opening of the *Agamemnon* of Æschylus the sentry set to watch for the beacon fire that is to announce the taking of Troy, sees at last the signal and sings at once of the victory and of his own release.

Judaism was a preparation for Jesus—building a road for Messiah's coming, straightening the paths, filling in the valleys, making the rough places smooth, that all flesh might see the salvation of God (3.3-6). Simeon is the representative of Israel welcoming the Messiah and handing over to Him. God's continuing missionary purpose through all the past ages led up to this hour, and it was His plan that now Judaism should pass away into the wider community of the Christian Church. Unhappily, though Simeon represented Judaism at its best, he did not represent its most characteristic expression at that hour—or perhaps at any hour.

In the Old Testament we may see again and again how the national pride and exclusive patriotism of the Jews struggled against the wider call of the Divine Spirit, how they tried to keep for a nation what God meant for mankind. The great prophets vehemently protested against such intolerance and narrowness; especially the one whom Simeon quotes in his song. The Second Isaiah united the two main themes in his message. God loves not only Israel but the Gentiles also and would have them brought to the knowledge of the truth. The truth about God is now known to Israel alone, and so Israel is to be His messenger to the world. As God has sent prophets to Israel so He sends Israel to the nations.

It is a commonplace of the Old Testament that Israel is the chosen people of Jehovah. To some even of the prophets this meant that Israel was Jehovah's spoilt child, dowered with the best He could give for its own pleasure and profit. But the Second Isaiah knew that Israel had been chosen not as God's favourite—He loved all nations —but as His servant; not instead of other nations but for their sakes. Israel had been chosen *because* God loved the world. As Israel had been marvellously redeemed from Egypt, so not less marvellously was it to be redeemed from the present captivity in Babylon. And by that deliverance it was to be enabled as a servant nation to win the world for God. ' It is too light a thing that thou shouldest be my servant to raise up the tribes of Jacob and to restore the preserved of Israel: I will also give thee for a light to the Gentiles that thou mayest be my salvation unto the end of the earth ' (Isa. 49.6).

Evidence that this great purpose had not been forgotten is to be found in one of the most popular Jewish books at the time of the birth of Christ, the Book of Enoch. Here is a sample quotation: ' And in my visions I saw that with the Eternal was one whose countenance was like man and his face full of graciousness. And I asked the angel and he said unto me, This is the Son of Man . . . And this Son of Man will be a staff to the righteous and a light to the Gentiles, and the hope of those who are troubled in heart. All who dwell on the earth shall bow the knee before him. For this reason he had been chosen before the foundation of the world and for evermore.'

Simeon believed that these remarkable words were now being fulfilled. Mary and Joseph were astonished at the old man's fervour and startling words. And to Mary he spoke words of profound insight. Salvation is to cost a heavy price in strife and suffering and opposition. ' This child is set for the falling and rising up of many in Israel and for a sign that is spoken against.' He will be the great test, He will bring men to the parting of the ways. By their response to the momentous choice He brings them they will be judged.

' The life of Christ has the decisiveness of a supreme

ideal, and that is why the history of the world divides at this point of time.'[1]

5

How many questions there are which we should like answered about the boyhood and youth of Jesus. The apocryphal Gospels have many worthless tales to offer, but the historical Gospels, in sharp contrast, have only one story—a simple, natural story, little likely to have been invented (2.41-52).

It was the custom of Joseph and Mary to go up once a year to Jerusalem for the Passover feast. The Law did not require the presence of women but the more devout often accompanied their husbands. This year the journey had a special significance. Jesus was twelve and at about that age a Jewish boy became a 'son of the law'; an event somewhat analogous to confirmation or 'joining the church'.

The story suggests, without precisely saying so, that this was His first visit since His infancy. The pilgrims went in a caravan (the meaning of the word translated 'company' in verse 44) made up of relations and neighbours. The excitement of the boys in the party must have been intense, and no doubt they would be on the move all the time from one party to another.

It was a great adventure for Jesus, this excursion into a larger world. The journey itself would be a delight. But how He must have thrilled when Jerusalem was reached, the ancient, historic capital of His people, and the city of the Temple. The Temple drew Him like a magnet. How much Jesus realized about Himself at this stage we cannot know, but we may perhaps see implicit in the story a strengthening, perhaps even a first awakening, of the sense of His great vocation. He shows at least an eager interest in divine things.

When His parents set off on the return journey, Jesus for some reason was not, as they supposed, in the caravan. It was a sign of their trust in Him that they did not feel the need to make sure. When they halted for the night His absence became clear. Much concerned they set off back to Jerusalem where at last on the third day they found Him

[1] A. N. Whitehead, *Religion in the Making*, p. 47.

in the Temple. Apparently surprised that His absence had caused any anxiety, He took it for granted that they would have known where He was. ' Did you not know that I must be in my Father's House? '

' Jesus disputing with the doctors,' some have called it. But the story tells only of an eager learning, a listening and an asking of questions. These learned rabbis in the Temple might perhaps be able to answer the questions He had asked in vain of the rabbi at Nazareth. This surely was for Jesus an hour of solemn dedication to the service of God.

He was already beyond the depth of Mary and Joseph. Looking back, as she told the story, the Mother found herself wondering at her repeated failures to understand (cf. verses 33, 48, 50). Yet Jesus went back with them obediently to the village home, continuing to grow and revealing in daily life a gracious personality.

In any picture we form of the education of Jesus that home must take a prominent place, with that Mother at the heart of it. One's imagination lingers on that home life with Jesus in the midst, and thinks sadly of the misunderstandings that clouded it later, when the family, no doubt moved by affectionate care for His well being, as they saw it, sought to restrain Him from His chosen task (8.19-21).

Such evidence as we have suggests that it was a home inspired by religious faith, of which the regular visits to the Temple were a symbol. It was there no doubt He learned the habit of regular attendance at the synagogue services (4.16). And probably we are not wrong in seeing in the many domestic pictures in the parables and sayings of Jesus reminiscences of the home He knew. There was cleaning (15.8) and baking and mending, and sometimes a garment that just would not stand another patch (5.36; cf. Mark 2.21). There were games with His companions in the village street. Only *a priori* assumptions could lead us to ignore the plain account of the brothers and sisters in the family. Joseph's name disappears early from the narrative. Perhaps he died and left Jesus as the eldest to support the home. Perhaps this was one reason why our Lord was not free to start His public ministry till the age of thirty.

School had also its part to play in His education. The Jews have always cared for learning. Jesus probably attended the synagogue school until He was sixteen or seventeen. The textbook would be the Scriptures and much of the study would consist in learning passages by heart along with a commentary. (Cf. 2 Tim. 3.15.) The mind of Jesus was richly stored with the treasures of the Old Testament. Deuteronomy and the Psalms, Hosea and Jeremiah, and especially the Second Isaiah, seem to have been best beloved by Him. His teaching has many references to them. He found in them light on His own calling; at moments of crisis their words came to Him in consolation and encouragement. The foundations of that knowledge and love of His Bible were laid in the village school.

Nature also spoke to Him. Nazareth is high on the hills looking out over plains steeped in historical associations. He loved the flowers. The scarlet anemones that carpet Galilee in spring like daisies in an English meadow were more lovely in His eyes than the purple robes of a king (12.27). He knew the ways of bird and beast, and the life of the farm. 'No words in the whole of antiquity are so full of appreciation of Nature as His.'[1]   His home was not far from the great caravan routes along which passed merchants, officials and soldiers.

Not least, perhaps, in His training was the discipline of the workshop. The mastery of any handicraft teaches lessons not to be found in books. The work of a village builder and carpenter, done as Jesus would do it, is rich in skill and variety and opportunities for human service.

Jesus grew physically and mentally as a normal boy does, yet with the grace, or favour, of God uniquely upon Him at every stage. He was a healthy vigorous boy endowed with singular spiritual gifts. The story of His life presents a man of great powers of physical and nervous endurance, for which a healthy boyhood must have prepared. He shared in the life of home and school and synagogue. Brief as our record is it sheds revealing light upon this whole process of growth and education.

[1] Otto Burchert, *The Original Jesus,* p. 203.

III

JESUS AND THE KINGDOM OF GOD

The Kingdoms of the Earth go by
  In purple and in gold;
They rise, they triumph, and they die,
  And all their tale is told.

One Kingdom only is divine,
  One banner triumphs still;
Its King a servant, and its sign
  A gibbet on a hill.

G. F. Bradby

WHEN John the Baptist appeared on the banks of the Jordan and proclaimed that the Kingdom of God was at hand, it was like setting a match to dry tinder. For the nation was in a mood of intense excitement and expectancy.

1

Throughout the Old Testament the promise is reiterated again and again that one day God will intervene to vindicate the right and to rescue His oppressed people. His Kingdom or Reign,[1] would become an obvious, living, present reality. The Day of the Lord, when God would act in power and with terrible all-embracing judgment, would transform the world into something new and glorious. The prophets often associated this Day with the doom of some oppressor of their own generation. In the time of Jesus it was the Romans against whom the patriots plotted. Many still cherished the memory of the great days of the revolt of the

---

[1] The word ' Kingdom ' is apt to suggest to us the misleading idea of a geographical territory like ' the United Kingdom of Great Britain and Northern Ireland '. The thought is rather of the Rule or Reign of God.

Maccabees and Rome had to deal with a turbulent people. In Jesus' youth the harsh suppression of a local rising in Galilee had intensified their hatred of the occupying power.

It is not surprising that many found their hearts beat faster as they read the militant words of the prophets and, looking back to the golden days of David and Solomon, dreamed of the restoration of the kingdom to Israel (Acts 1.6). Peacemakers were suspect. The violent who tried to take the Kingdom of God by force were the popular heroes. To suggest that Caesar had any rights at all was to lay oneself open to suspicion.

But there were also those who dwelt instead upon other elements in the message of the prophets. They rejected the way of revolution and called for a more scrupulous observance of the divine Law: it was for God, not man, to bring in the Kingdom. Many who thought like this found their faith expressed in the so-called 'apocalyptic' books. The word literally means 'revelation', and gives no clue to their contents. Some idea of their character may be gathered from the two representatives of this literature in the Bible, *Daniel* and *Revelation,* or *'The Apocalypse of St. John the Divine'.* Many volumes, characterized by much the same outlook and couched in similar visionary and symbolic language, appeared over a period of some three centuries before and after the time of Christ; roughly speaking, between 200 B.C. and A.D. 100.

The apocalyptists had lost faith in redemption by the turn of political events. Politics was bankrupt. Instead they sought to hearten men by the assurance that God Himself would intervene. The catastrophic collapse of the existing order would be the prelude to a glorious future. With all its bizarre accompaniments, apocalyptic expressed a magnificent faith in the power and goodness of God, refusing to admit that the last word was with evil and oppression.

There was a turmoil of controversy about the Kingdom, and no doubt many were uncertain what to think. But at least there was agreement that *something* had got to happen.

So when John the Baptist declared that the Kingdom of God was at hand and summoned the nation to prepare itself by repentance and dedication, he met with an instant response. The people flocked to hear him and many offered themselves for his symbolic rite of baptism in the Jordan

(3.1-20). Patriotism and religion combined to make men listen. His dominating personality started a movement which lasted right through New Testament times and later. He was a greater figure than the casual reader of the Gospels is apt to realize. (See, e.g. Acts 18.24-28; 19.1-7.)

2

We cannot, of course, know what was happening in the mind and heart of Jesus in the eighteen years since He was about His Father's business in the Temple. But we cannot be wrong in surmising much thought and prayer as to God's will for the world. When John preached, the soul of Jesus responded, and He too offered Himself for baptism, to associate Himself with this mission of repentance and hope (3.21-22).

The account of what happened at the baptism must have come in part at least from Jesus Himself. It is the record of an intense experience, of an inner voice speaking with imperious authority in His heart, of a new consciousness of spiritual power.[1] Perhaps there came to Him then a fuller knowledge of unique relationship to the Father and a call to a unique task. It seems probable that the baptismal experience set the seal on convictions that had been gathering strength in His mind. 'Thou art my beloved son: in thee I am well pleased.' (See Ps. 2.7; Isa. 42.1.)

Jesus had long pondered the Old Testament ideals. Now at this great moment these two passages spoke to Him with convincing, individualizing authority. He Himself was called to be the Messiah of the psalmist and the Servant of the prophet, united in one. The baptism was an experience of divine calling and endowment with power. It lies behind all the future words and deeds of Jesus in the Gospel story.

3

From Jesus Himself must also have come the story of the following days of strain and trial in the wilderness where in loneliness He faced the full meaning of His baptismal

---

[1] Mark and Matthew explicitly say that the descent of the dove was a personal vision of Jesus, and none of the Gospels say that the voice was heard or the dove seen by any other.

experience (4.1-13). Perhaps it was at Caesarea Philippi that He told His disciples about it, when He drew from them a recognition of His Messiahship but had to make it clear that His conception of the role was very different from the popular one. Perhaps it was then He told them how on the threshold of His work He had rejected the plans and hopes they still cherished, as nothing less than temptations of the devil.

The story is told in the parabolic form which was His customary way of speaking of spiritual things: it is a symbolic account of inward struggle. To interpret the story literally would be to make it grotesque. Even if we could accept the idea of a personal evil spirit actually appearing and could conceive of Jesus being carried bodily through the air to a high mountain to view the kingdoms of the world, there is of course no mountain from which they could be seen. Nor would an obvious appeal to worship a present devil be any temptation to such as Jesus. His victory consisted precisely in the recognition of these suggested plans of action as fundamentally evil, in seeing that they would lead to the devil's kingdom not to God's.

The symbolism has been very variously interpreted, but it is most natural to understand it as the facing of the implications of His call to Messiahship.[1]

The first temptation clearly has many possible interpretations along other lines, as, for example, a temptation to use divine power for selfish ends, to meet His own hunger. Or perhaps it was a reaction after the great spiritual experience of the baptism, the insinuation of a doubt as to its reality. ' *If* thou be the Son of God, test it by calling upon the power of God to turn stones into bread. Ask God for a sign.' One may recall how John Bunyan in distress as to whether or no he possessed saving faith was tempted one day between Elstow and Bedford to demand a sign from God—to say to the puddles be dry and to the dry places be puddles.

But let us look at it rather as the suggestion of a possible way to the Kingdom of God, which Jesus rejected. Why should He not make the provision of bread His life work? Jesus knew what hunger was and His sympathy with the

---

[1] An illuminating commentary on the Temptation is given in the Grand Inquisitor's speech in *The Brothers Karamazov* by Dostoevsky, Book V, Chapter 5.

poor is reflected in every page of the Gospel. ' I was an hungered and ye gave me no meat ': He can think of no severer condemnation. The tragic poverty around must have cried out for all His help. And if He were to set Himself to meet the physical necessities of men would He not gain their allegiance for His teaching?

The Fourth Gospel records that when compassion moved Him to feed a crowd they wanted to make Him their king on the spot (John 6.1-15). But that was because they wanted loaves and fishes, not because they wanted the Kingdom of God. And Jesus withdrew from them. It was not that He thought feeding the hungry a bad thing—far from it; but it was not the same thing as the Kingdom of God. ' Jesus,' it has been said, ' would have been the last to fling a text to a starving man.' But there are times when a word of God is more precious than bread, when hunger and privation are in the path of duty. A Gospel of social reform that cared for men's bodies and forgot their spirits would be as alien to the Christian Faith as one that cared nothing for men's bodies while seeking to save their souls. Real men and women are soul and body; yet the true business of living only begins when our physical needs are satisfied. Man needs bread, yet not by bread alone shall man live, but by every word that proceedeth out of the mouth of God.

The Second Temptation suggests an even closer relation to popular expectations. The people were ready to give enthusiastic support to one who would take the lead, as the response to John's preaching had shown. It is true their dominant desire was vengeance on Rome, but after all Rome was a barrier in the way. Once power was gained it could be used to lead the people to higher ideas. Men do not win kingdoms by preaching. Why not throw in your lot with the Zealots? Raise the standard of revolt like the Maccabees—and the kingdom is yours.

No, said Jesus. To accept the alliance of evil in the establishment of the Kingdom, to let the end justify the means—that is nothing less than the worship of the devil.

If the second temptation thus suggested alliance with the Zealots, perhaps the Third was a suggestion of alliance with the Pharisees. They rejected the way of revolution as futile. Wait for God to take the initiative, they said. He will act in His own way and at His own time. If men would hasten His Kingdom it could only be by the scrupulous observance of His Law. Nothing but a supernatural act of God could usher in the new divine order.

'The Lord whom ye seek shall suddenly come to His Temple,' says a verse in Malachi (3.1), and Daniel saw 'one like the Son of Man coming with the clouds of heaven' (7.13). Jesus imagined Himself as descending among the thronging worshippers in the Temple courts and pictured them crowding around to hail Him as the Messiah. A startling visible sign, in line with their expectations, might be the way to win the people.

Explain it how we will, and the subject is discussed in a later chapter, there is no doubt that Jesus believed Himself to possess powers of control over nature, and that His contemporaries acknowledged His power. This was a real temptation. It looked like a short cut to the Kingdom—as if the long road of misunderstanding and rejection which He must have seen ahead as at least a possible outcome of His mission, might be avoided. But such a bludgeoning of men's senses would have no moral value. If they could not read the divine message in His person there could be no other sign for them.

It would have been possible for Jesus to turn social reformer and to better the lot of many. It would have been possible to adopt the role of the warrior Christ, and to establish Himself as king at Jerusalem. It would have been possible to exploit the apocalyptic expectations of the day and win allegiance by irrational and unspiritual devices. But the heart and will cannot be compelled, they can only be won. He would be neither Wonder Worker nor Warrior, but Son and Servant. There was no short cut to the Kingdom, no easy way of establishing the rule of God.

Whatever more the Temptation may mean, at least it represents the definite renunciation of the political conception of the Messianic vocation.

4

At the outset of the public career of Jesus, Luke records a detailed account of His appearance in the synagogue at Nazareth (4.14-30). It must have been a moving occasion for everybody. Many memories would throng upon Jesus Himself as He entered the synagogue. This was His home town. He had worshipped in this synagogue for some thirty years. It had been His school as well as His church. His teachers were no doubt present, perhaps His mother, and certainly many of the companions of His boyhood and youth. They must have watched with a lively curiosity, as He came forward to read and to speak. 'The eyes of all in the synagogue were fastened on Him.' The account is so full of drama and of life-like detail that it must surely have come to Luke from someone who was there.

It is not certain if the passage Jesus read was chosen by Him or was the reading for the day. A lectionary determined the choice of the first lesson, from the Law, but it has not been proved that the lectionary which was later adopted for the second lesson, from the prophets, had come into force by this date. It is hard to say which would be the more remarkable: that Jesus should choose this passage out of all the prophets as text for His sermon; or that a divine coincidence should have made it the regular lesson for this momentous Sabbath. No doubt he read a longer passage, and in fact Luke has here run together two neighbouring quotation. (Isa. 61.1; 58.6.)

As Jesus finished reading and rolled up the scroll and gave it to the attendant, and then in accordance with custom sat down to speak, there was a hush of universal attention. Here was someone they knew well: and yet He was somehow different from the youth they had known. (There is a hint in verse 14 of a new spiritual strength gained through the experiences of the Baptism and the Temptation.) Perhaps there had been a new note in the way He read the familiar passage—with authority, with conviction, with appropriation as if the words were His own.

The report of His address is no doubt a summary. He reminded them that this passage was a declaration of God's eternal missionary purpose. God had been doing these gracious deeds in all generations—so far as men would let Him. The initiative had been with God. He sent the prophets and the healers. Now Jesus claimed to be carrying forward this divine plan: God has consecrated *me* to preach this Gospel. But Jesus does more than claim a place among the prophets. This is the hour of the accomplish-

ment of the promises of God: to-day is this Scripture fulfilled.

At first the congregation is delighted and impressed. He
spoke with charm. 'Gracious words' means graciousness
in delivery and manner, though it may also contain a reference to the subject matter: 'gracious words about the grace
of God'. But as the sermon progressed anger took the
place of approval. For Jesus touched Jewish national pride
at its most sensitive spot.

God's message, He declared, was for all men. Often in
the past His goodness had been extended to foreigners like
the widow of Sarepta and Naaman. Often it had been rejected by the Jews. The anger of His audience makes it
clear that Jesus was not emphasizing already accepted
truths when He proclaimed that men should come from
the east and west, and from the north and south to sit down
in the kingdom of God (13.29). The great prophets had
sometimes taught this, but it was new and unwelcome to the
generation of Jesus.[1]

The congregation were so angry that they wanted to lynch
Him and anticipate Calvary. We need not attribute His
escape to any miraculous cause, except the miracle of His
personality. It was the power of a calm and brave spirit
that overawed them; a power that Wesley and George Fox
and others possessed in their measure. There are other
similar stories in the Gospels. (Cf. John 7.44-46; 18.3-6.)

5

In some of the prophets and apocalyptic books the coming of the Kingdom is associated with a 'Messiah' or
'Christ', an 'anointed' servant of God, sometimes identi-
fied with a contemporary hero, sometimes pictured as a
supernatural figure. Judging from the Synoptic Gospels,
Jesus at the outset of His ministry made no open claim to
be the Messiah: no doubt because of the political and
revolutionary associations of the word in many minds. The
turning point of the ministry came when the inner group
of disciples nevertheless recognized Him as indeed the
Messiah. 'Thou art the Christ of God!' said Peter. Even
then Jesus commanded them to keep this secret. He was

[1] In spite of emphasis in some of the current apocalyptic books.

not yet ready to make a public claim. His Messiahship was very different from the popular idea. Suffering not conquest lay ahead. The Messiah was to be the suffering Servant of mankind, not its domineering conqueror. He was not to wade through slaughter to His throne, but take the way of rejection and the Cross (9.18-22).

When He came to Jerusalem to make His last appeal to His people, Jesus dramatically fulfilled an ancient prophecy of the King who came to reign, riding upon an ass instead of a war horse. ' And he shall speak peace unto the nations: and his dominion shall be from sea to sea and from the River to the ends of the earth ' (Zech. 9.9-10). That was the kind of Messiah He was.

6

We must try now in the light of these incidents to summarize what the Gospel has to say about three issues of fundamental importance in the message and work of Jesus; (1) the coming of the Kingdom of God, (2) the place of Jesus Himself in the Kingdom and (3) the universal range of the Kingdom.

(1) At Nazareth, as we have seen, Jesus declared that the Day had arrived. The decisive hour had struck. The Reign of God had come (4.21). This claim that the Kingdom of God was already in being was one of the keynotes of the preaching of Jesus throughout His ministry.

When John the Baptist asked ' Art thou he that should come? ', that is, the Messiah, the answer pointed to the visible signs of the powers of the Kingdom (7.18-23). John, greatest among men as he is, is less than the least in the Kingdom. To him it was only a hope. Now the privileges of the Kingdom are available to all (7.28; cf. 16.16).

When the seventy returned with joyful reports of the success of their mission, Jesus cried: Blessed are the eyes which see the things which you see, for you see what prophets and kings longed to see, the actual arrival of the Kingdom (10.23-24; 10.9-11). ' If I by the finger of God cast out demons, then is the Kingdom of God come upon you! ' (11.20).

The saying ' The Kingdom of God is within you ' (17.21) is difficult to interpret. The word almost certainly means

' within ', not ' among '; Luke uses a different Greek expression seven times elsewhere when he clearly means ' among '. The difficulty is that the saying is addressed to Pharisees, but perhaps ' you ' has a general meaning. The sense is that the Kingdom of God is an inward and spiritual reality rather than outward and visible. But however the saying be interpreted, it does at least assert that the Kingdom is now present.

The Kingdom is now present. Yet there are other passages where the Kingdom is apparently still in process of coming, as in the parables of the mustard seed and the leaven. Others again clearly assert that the Kingdom is still in the future. He taught the disciples to pray that the Kingdom might come (11.2). There is a mysterious saying in the story of the Last Supper (22.18) which speaks of the Kingdom in the future. And there are enigmatic sayings which seem to foretell a sudden miraculous coming when the Kingdom will shine out instantaneously like the lightning; will, as it were, spring upon men in the midst of their work and pleasure (12.35-40; 17.26-36). He speaks of the strain upon faith caused by long delay (12.45; 18.6-8). In one passage (19.11) Luke is apparently anxious to correct the impression that Jesus declared that the Kingdom of God was about to come.

It is all rather perplexing, and attempts have frequently been made by scholars with ' either—or ' minds to eliminate one or other strain in the teaching. But both are there. We need not decide that the two conceptions as Jesus taught them were really in opposition. They are different aspects of truth about the Kingdom rather than incompatible points of view. The Kingdom is here and now, and yet it is still to come. It was incarnate in Jesus. It comes as men and women one by one yield themselves to the rule of God and as they try to secure the expression of God's will in society. There will be a culmination, a climax, a coming of Christ in power. Come, coming, still to come: it is the paradox of the Kingdom.

From time to time it is necessary to remind oneself that Jesus was not delivering theological lectures or answering the precise queries of legal minds. He spoke in the poetic symbolical language of the Hebrew prophet. He was never giving prosaic calculations about dates. At times He spoke in the language of exultation as if in the prospect of immediate triumph. At other times He looked out with calm foresight upon the future.

The twenty-first chapter, with its parallels in Mark 13 and Matthew 24, presents us with perhaps the most difficult of all problems in the interpretation of the Gospels. It is a long discourse about the future, unlike anything else in the Gospels, and closely resembling contemporary Jewish apocalyptic writings. Whatever view be taken difficulties remain unsolved. Which of the three versions is nearest to what Jesus said? Did Jesus ever speak some of the sayings at all? Have we here a Jewish or Jewish-Christian apocalypse in which some sayings of Jesus are incorporated? If we do accept one of the reports as accurate, how are we to interpret it?

Plainly we cannot rely upon having here the exact words of Jesus and we must not build doctrine on any single phrase in one account. The greater part of the chapter admittedly refers to the destruction of Jerusalem which took place in A.D. 70 when Titus razed the city to the ground. But it is very difficult to disentangle the references to the fall of Jerusalem from the references to what is usually called the Second Coming. The doom of Jerusalem is thrown against a richly coloured Eastern background of cosmic portents. Literalism is out of place. We must recognize also that aspects of our Lord's teaching most in accord with current ideas would be most emphasized and that therefore teaching furthest from contemporary notions is most likely to be authentic. It is notable that in Matthew and Mark the whole passage closes with the emphatic declaration that Jesus was ignorant of the time of His return (Mark 13.32; Matt. 24.36; cf. Acts. 1.6-7).

We may perhaps sum up by saying that Jesus spoke of the Kingdom as already present but that He also looked forward to a consummation associated with Himself, which He described in the language of His race and age, not intended to be interpreted literally. It is beyond question that the first generations of the Church lived in constant anticipation of a spectacular return of Christ to establish His Kingdom. There must have been some elements in His teaching, however much misunderstood, to give rise to such an expectation. There is no clear indication that He ex-

pected this Return to be in the lifetime of His own generation. Equally it cannot be asserted that He looked forward
to centuries of development. He said Himself that He did
not know the time. Perhaps the time is uncertain and dependent in part upon human response. Perhaps the coming
of the Kingdom waits upon the faith of men. Jesus knew
the Kingdom would certainly come in full triumph but He
did not know the day. To attempt to work out ' times and
seasons ' from the Bible is a waste of time and a plain
misunderstanding of the teaching of Jesus.[1]

(2) Jesus not only proclaimed the coming of the Kingdom
as a prophet might do. He declared that it had come in
Himself. In Jewish terminology, He was the Messiah, the
divinely appointed inaugurator of the Kingdom. When
Peter acknowledged Him as the Messiah, Jesus accepted
the title and according to Matthew's version commended
Peter for his divinely inspired insight (Luke 9.18-21; Matt.
16.13-20).

Jesus interpreted His vocation as Messiah in terms of the
Son of Man of the Book of Daniel, and of the Servant of the
Lord of the Second Isaiah, the author of Isaiah 40-55. A
full discussion would take us far beyond the possible limits
of this book. Both conceptions seem originally related to
a community rather than to an individual. In the Book of
Daniel (chapter 7) Israel appears after the domineering
militaristic kingdom symbolized by beasts, as by contrast
a human kingdom like unto *a* son of man, representative
of the saints of the Most High. But in later Jewish thought,
in the *Similitudes of Enoch* and elsewhere, this personifica-
tion of Israel apparently became a title of the Messiah.
Scholars are still vigorously disputing the meaning of the
phrase whether in Jewish thought or in the use made of it
by Jesus. Perhaps He used the title Son of Man just because of its vagueness and mystery, as one into which He
could put His own content.

In Second Isaiah again, in the series of Servant Songs
(Isa. 42.1-4; 49.1-6; 50.4-9; 52.13-53.12) it seems that the
prophet is portraying the ideal Israel as it responded to the
divine calling. Yet it is difficult to believe that, especially

---

[1] I have used here material from my booklet, *The Necessity of
the Second Coming* (S.C.M. Press) in which I have discussed the
whole subject at much greater length.

in chapter 53, the writer had not some individual before his mind's eye as a model. This chapter was not regarded as a Messianic picture by Jewish theologians, which makes all the more remarkable its selection by Jesus. His identification of Himself with the Servant lies behind His sermon at Nazareth and His references to His death. The only direct quotation in Luke is in 22.37, but there is almost certainly a reference in the unexpected phrase ' a ransom for *many* ', (Matt. 20.25-28; Mark 10.42-45; cf. Luke 22.25-27) with its reminiscence of ' justify many ' and ' bare the sin of many ' (Isa. 53.11-12). To understand Jesus the Kingdom must never be separated from the Cross. The Messiah—impossible thought as it was to the Jews—had to die. But the Cross came not because of His defeat by His enemies in church and state but as a deliberately chosen path; chosen and made necessary because of the opposition and sin of men.

It is clear, therefore, that if Jesus took up and even to some extent shared the hopes and longings of His countrymen, He also transformed them. The conception of the Kingdom of God was a framework to be filled with His own meaning, building upon the nobler elements in the great prophetic teachings and yet giving to it all His own unique content. His message of the Kingdom differed just to the extent that His message about God was different. The Kingdom on earth was to be the realized will of God, and God was as Jesus made Him known. His will was for forgiveness and reconciliation; peace with Himself and peace among His children. The love of God was even now to be seen at work in His world, clothing the grass and feeding the sparrows and caring for all His children. But the advent of His rule in its fulness would mean the complete downfall of Satan, author both of moral evil and of disease. It would mean the transformation of the world and not its destruction, as the apocalyptists held. Fundamentally the Kingdom was the willingly accepted sovereignty of God in the hearts and lives of men and women; a changed relationship to God, bringing with it a changed relationship to one another.

(3) The Kingdom of God as Jesus proclaimed it and embodied it was a universal Kingdom open to all men at the same price. It was not the Jewish preserve believed in by

most of His contemporaries. One of the glories of Luke's
Gospel is that it brings out this universal mission of Jesus
more clearly than the others. Even in Matthew's Gospel,
the most Jewish of them all, we see a Christ who is more
than a Jew. Mark's Gospel shows the conflict of the wider
outlook of Jesus with the traditions of Judaism, dramatically ending with the rending of the veil of the Temple and
the confession of the pagan centurion. But Luke's two-
volume book opens with the aged Simeon pronouncing the
epitaph of Judaism as a nobler faith still, a faith for Gentiles
as well as Jews, is taking its place. Then at once Luke sets
his story against the wider horizons of the Roman world
(3.1). Again and again in the Gospel the same note is
struck. In Acts Luke rejoices to tell of the admission of
Gentiles to equal rights in the Church. At the end Paul is
in Rome and the Church is firmly planted at the centre of
the world.

It is characteristic of him that Luke alone records the
references to God's care for foreigners in the sermon at
Nazareth (4.25-27). He traces the genealogy of Jesus not
only to Abraham as Matthew does, but right back to Adam
(3.38). He has much to say of the relations of Jesus with
the Samaritans, with whom Jews had characteristically no
dealings (John 4.9; see 9.52-56; 10.30-37; 17.16).

Jesus disentangled religion from its national setting. His
appeal was as wide as humanity. His message about God's
Kingdom and the conditions of entrance contains nothing
to make it Jewish (cf. 13.28-30). The Beatitudes say nothing
about racial qualifications and the Lord's Prayer voices the
needs and aspirations of every man. There is nothing
national about the stories of the Prodigal Son and the Good
Samaritan. Indeed the latter explicitly sets the claims of
human need above the prejudices of creed and nationality.

The Kingdom of God in the teaching of Jesus is a
profoundly religious conception: not the political Jewish
triumph of many of His contemporaries, nor yet the social
Utopia imagined by many moderns. The Kingdom does
not come by the inevitable processes of evolutionary history,
but neither does it come by divine fiat. Jesus' call to prayer
for its coming and for penitence and effort show that more
than passive expectancy is asked from men. It is of the
essence of it that men and women receive it willingly with

heart and mind and strength. We are to pray for its coming (11.2). We are to seek it (12.31). It is to be entered (18.24). It is the gift of God and yet it is a gift to be sought. There is a task to be done. Of course we cannot perform God's part, and yet no less a Christian than the apostle Paul tells us that we are to be His fellow workers. The prayer and response of men could affect the time and manner in which it would be possible for God to give them the Kingdom. Jesus called men not to fatalism but to willing alliance with the divine purpose. The Kingdom is the gift of God received by the faith of man.

IV

JESUS AND PRAYER

. . . Fervent love,
And lively hope, with violence assail
The Kingdom of the Heavens, and overcome
The will of the Most High; not in such sort
As man prevails o'er man; but conquers it,
Because 'tis willing to be conquered; still,
Though conquered, by its mercy, conquering.
Dante *Paradiso*, Canto XX.   Carey's translation

JESUS lived by faith in God. That was the secret of everything. He 'went about doing good', but service was no substitute for prayer. God was to Him the supreme Reality: He lived as seeing Him who is invisible. Yet this world of space and time was none the less entirely real also. We do not see Him truly unless we see both service and prayer to be equally parts of His life. Each depended upon the other.

The background of His life and the inspiration of all His actions was His fellowship with the Father. The unseen spiritual world was as familiar as the lanes of Galilee and the streets of Jerusalem. The Kingdom of God was more real than the empire of Caesar. We see Him seeking relief and refreshment of spirit from the pressure of the world's pain and need in quiet retirement on the hills and moors. When there are hard problems to face and hard paths to tread He finds guidance and strength in prayer.

The later Church was troubled by the prayers of Jesus. Jesus was God. Could God pray to God? It was suggested that only His human nature prayed, not His divine; so denying His true humanity. But the Gospels are unconscious of such problems. It is enough for them to record the facts and to leave it to later generations to explain them, which perhaps they have not yet fully done.

Luke in particular was impressed by the sight of Jesus at prayer. He has collected and treasured more about His teaching and practice here than any other Gospel. Seven instances of Jesus at prayer are recorded by Luke alone, and he alone preserved some of the parables about prayer. This same concern with prayer is to be seen in his later volume, The Acts.

1

In the life of Jesus there was a regular rhythm of work and prayer. He made a practice of withdrawing to some quiet country spot to pray (e.g. 4.42; cf. Mark 1.35). Perhaps it was an old habit of his youth; privacy and quiet must have been difficult to find in the full little home. After days when teaching and healing had made great demands upon spiritual and physical strength He would retire by Himself as evening fell (5.15-16). The virtue that went out of Him (6.19; 8.46) as He poured out His sympathy to those in distress or healed the sick or wrestled with the needs of some evil-ridden soul, was restored to Him in quiet communion with the Father. But Jesus spoke also of the value of corporate prayer (cf. Matt. 18.19-20) and Luke tells us that it was His custom to join, Sabbath by Sabbath, in the worship of the synagogue (4.16,31,44; 6.6; 13.10).

In addition to these regular practices of private and corporate prayer, Luke tells us how Jesus gave Himself specially to prayer as He confronted the great crises of His life.

It was in prayer that Jesus consecrated Himself to His mission. Luke alone tells us that the Holy Spirit descended as Jesus was praying when He came up streaming out of the waters of His baptism (3.21-22). It was after an all-night vigil that He made His momentous choice of the twelve apostles (6.12). Again we are told that He prayed before presenting His challenge to the twelve and drawing from them the acknowledgement of His Messiahship (9.18). Perhaps, as suggested in the last chapter, it was then that He first told them the story of His Temptation, in explaining to them what kind of Messiah He was—so different from the popular picture. It was a familiar enough sight under Roman rule in Palestine to see condemned men going to execution carrying the beam of their cross upon their shoulder. It was like that—not with banners waving but

D

carrying a cross—that they must follow Him. It was a call not to self-denial of the luxuries of life, but to dangerous, adventurous living, ready like Him at any moment to lay down their lives so that God's Kingdom might come. So high was the cost of loyalty.

But there was a reward of loyalty too, to see before long signal evidence of the advance of God's Kingdom—a mysterious promise, of which the reference is not clear. Some say Jesus spoke of the Transfiguration, about a week later. Others say He meant His Resurrection, or Pentecost, or the great missionary expansion of the early Church, or the Fall of Jerusalem.

With the shadow of the Cross lying clearly athwart His path Jesus came to the hill of the Transfiguration. It must have been an hour of great heart searching. Again only Luke tells us that it was in the act of prayer that Jesus was transfigured and His face became radiant with an inner light. The Transfiguration experience, we may gather from the Gospel, meant both renewed self-dedication and Divine reassurance. Through prayer He received the encouragement and strength He sought (9.28-36).

And when the Cross was close at hand, again He sought solitude and the company of His nearest friends (22.39-46). One shrinks from speculating about the meaning of Gethsemane. That figure prostrate in deep distress of soul calls for silence and reverence. Hungry for the sympathy His three companions were unable to give, He yet had to go farther on into the dark shadow of the garden by Himself to pour out His soul to the Father. He knew now to the full the bitterness of the cup filled for Him by human sin: betrayal, desertion, the Cross: suffering of soul and suffering of body. How dreadful to Him must have been the deep perversion of personality that could respond to His offer of love by hatred and crucifixion. ' He came unto His own, and His own received Him not.' There is more here than the shrinking from a violent and torturing death—though the bravest of men know that. ' The chastisement of our sins was upon Him.'

' Father, if thou be willing, remove this cup from me: nevertheless not my will, but thine, be done.' His shrinking did not overcome His steadfast readiness to do the Father's will, cost what it might.

Knowing the trial His disciples were about to endure He urged them to prayer, and it was in prayer that He Himself faced this hour of sorrow and desolation. Some texts of Luke's Gospel say that an angel appeared to Him, strengthening Him. Certainly strength came from heaven, and calm after the storm.

He prayed too upon the Cross itself. Luke tells us of two specific acts of prayer. He prayed for His murderers. Where from another one might have expected entreaties for mercy, cries of pain, hot abuse and denunciation, from Him came only this: ' Father, forgive them, for they know not what they do ' (23.34). Nineteen hundred years later in a Japanese prison cell a brutal Japanese murderer and all-round scoundrel read those words and was shaken out of his callousness into a new life. (See *A Gentleman in Prison*. Macdonald.) It is a word that pierces.

Luke records also that the last breath of Jesus was a prayer: ' Father into thy hands I commend my spirit ' (23.46). It is a quotation from a Psalm (31.5). Other words from the Cross suggest that during those hours of pain Jesus was repeating psalms to Himself. Much light is thrown upon that terrible and baffling cry: ' My God, my God, why hast thou forsaken me ' (Mark 15.34) when we realize that it too is a quotation from a Psalm (22) and when we read it in its context.

2

The sight of Jesus at prayer made His disciples ask Him to teach them to pray (11.1). No doubt they had prayed before, but they found that the prayers of Jesus were different. The consideration of His prayers makes us too want to turn to His teaching about prayer. In the Lord's Prayer we have an inexhaustible lesson. Here is not ' much speaking ' but brevity and directness; yet the longer these few words are studied the more are depths beyond depths revealed.

It will be seen that the Revised Version of Luke 11.1-4 gives a much shorter text of the Lord's Prayer than does the Authorized. Scholars are agreed that the shorter one is the one that stood originally in Luke's Gospel and that the additions were made by copyists who tended to assimilate it to the longer version in Matthew's Gospel. It is likely that two versions were in oral circulation in the early Church.

As the Revised Version gives it, the Lord's Prayer in Luke's account reads thus: 'Father, hallowed be thy name. Thy kingdom come. Give us day by day our daily bread. And forgive us our sins: for we ourselves also forgive everyone that is indebted to us. And bring us not into temptation.'

The Fatherhood of God is the presupposition of all Christian prayer, and the very heart of Christian belief. Abba, Father, was Jesus' characteristic way of addressing God and thinking about Him. At the very beginning of His ministry the voice from heaven at the baptism reveals that in that creative experience it was as Father that He thought of God. And so it was, the Gospel assures us, in all the most intimate experiences of His life, right up to the prayer in Gethsemane and His last word on the Cross. Jesus knew Himself to stand in a peculiar relationship to God. But He claims also, through what He is and does, to bring others to know God as Father. By being the Son He makes known the nature of the Father (10.21-22).

The name was not new. Like all the phrases in the Lord's Prayer it can be paralleled from Jewish sources. 'Father' is indeed a not unusual way of addressing God in prayer in early Judaism: though some scholars maintain that it was not common before the time of Christ. But it is certainly true that when Jesus said 'Father' an altogether new warmth and significance was given to the word, and that it opened a transforming era in men's thoughts of God. Jesus did something to the familiar word. For Him Father was not just a name for God: it was the expression of the ruling conviction of His life. The newness and power of His revelation of God's Fatherhood can be felt thrilling through such a passage as Romans 8.12-39.

To study the Lord's Prayer is to learn to know not only prayer but God Himself. It summarizes the teaching of Jesus about the divine Fatherhood, and it never allows us to forget that all Christian prayer is offered not by isolated souls but by children in a family to the Father of the family. The health and peace of the world depend upon our learning that.

(1) The Father is Lord of heaven and earth, of nations and of men. Man's chief end is to glorify Him and enjoy Him for ever. Reverence and obedience are the first words of prayer. *Hallowed be thy name:* May the Father be known everywhere and worshipped as He truly is. May our light so shine before men that they may see our good works and glorify our Father in heaven (Matt. 5.16).

Thy Kingdom come: thy reign begin. Luke, according to the best manuscripts, does not add ' thy will be done on earth as it is in heaven ', but that is the meaning. This comes first: personal needs come later. And indeed it is only as we seek first the Kingdom that our true needs can be met. Of all that the Kingdom meant to Jesus we have tried to speak elsewhere.

(2) The Father cares for each of His children.

Give us day by day our daily bread. The Father knows that we have need of food and drink and clothing (12.30). In the bounty of nature He has made provision for all. But it is *our* bread: if the children quarrel and snatch at the family table then all will suffer and some may starve. ' We ' are all the children of God throughout the world, and we pray for the satisfaction of, let us say, the needs of Displaced Persons in Germany and Indian peasants not less than our own.

The precise meaning of the Greek word translated ' daily ' is an unsolved mystery. But it seems likely that it means ' bread enough for the coming day ': our needful rations as it were.

Jesus never forgets that men are body and soul: not soul only. God cares for the whole man.

Forgive us our sins, for we ourselves also forgive everyone that is indebted to us. Forgiveness is our fundamental spiritual need, as bread is our fundamental physical need.

The forgiveness of others is not the condition on which God is willing to forgive us, so much as an inevitable necessity of the spiritual world. The unforgiving man is incapable of being restored to that fellowship with God which is forgiveness (1 John 4.20).

' Our sins ' include those corporate sins of society where we share in the common guilt, like war and prostitution. In penitence as well as in petition we come before God as part of His family.

And bring us not into temptation. The children need guidance and protection: God will give it. This clause is not concerned with the source from which temptation comes, but with the need for protection against it. But it might be misinterpreted, and it has been. It was probably with mis-understandings of the Lord's Prayer in mind that James wrote: ' Let no man say when he is tempted, I am tempted of God: for God cannot be tempted with evil, neither tempteth he any man ' (James 1.13). Only good can come from God.

3

Luke records three parables that reinforce this teaching about prayer. The first he puts immediately after the Lord's Prayer (11.5-8). It is a vivid picture of Eastern village life. An argument is being carried on between a man outside a locked door, and a man in bed with his family around him in the one room of the little cottage. The man outside explains that a friend has arrived unexpectedly and there is nothing in the larder. He has come to borrow some bread. But the man in bed is sleepy and surly. He cannot be bothered to get up. It is too difficult to open the door and anyhow he might wake the children. As if they could be sleeping through all the knocking and shouting! But the beggar will not take no for an answer and with an ill grace and just so as to get rid of him the man gets out of bed in the end and sends him away with his loaves.

Well, suggests Jesus, if importunity gets results out of such an unlikely person as that, what can you not count on when you approach your Father who is ready and willing to help. Ask and you will get. If asking is not enough, seek: do something about it. Put yourself behind your request. And if need be keep on knocking till the door opens (11.9-10). ' Longing desire prayeth always though the tongue be silent,' wrote Augustine. ' If thou art ever longing thou art ever praying. When stayeth prayer? When desire groweth cold.'

Ordinary human fathers for all their faults can be trusted to give their children honest food and not useless or poisonous stuff. You can learn about your heavenly Father from watching earthly fathers. But God is infinitely better than the best of them (11.9-13). At its best, earthly father-hood is but a faint reflection of God (Eph. 3.14-15; Jas. 1.17).

Luke records another parable of contrast, also commend-ing importunity (18.1-8): ' to the end that they ought always to pray and not to faint '—or lose heart. A cynical scoundrel of a judge sees justice done to a defenceless widow, because she keeps on pestering him. ' She'll be giving me a black eye next, if I don't look out! ' is the sense of verse 5. (Again there is the touch of humour that ap-peared in the story of the surly man in bed.)

Over tried faith sometimes pictures God as indifferent and unjust. Why does God not stop the war, or some other obvious evil? Why is injustice allowed to triumph? Doesn't God care?

God, said Jesus, is as unlike an unjust judge as you can imagine. You can rely upon Him to do the right as speedily and effectively as it can be done. There are good reasons for His apparent delay. The real obstacle to the coming of His Reign is not in Him but in men. When He does act will He find men ready? Is there loyal confidence enough in the world? There almost seems a hint of weariness and sadness in the words.

Somehow our prayers help to prepare the way for God. Prayer is not overcoming His reluctance but making it possible for Him to do what He longs to do.

There follows a third parable of prayer which Luke alone records: the story of the Pharisee and the Publican (18.9-14).

The Pharisee, apparently praying but really talking to himself (verse 11), is passing a vote of confidence in his own piety and worthiness. He congratulates himself on his per-fect respectability, and on surpassing all legal demands in his religious devotion. What a contrast to that wretched tax gatherer over there! It is a scandal they allow men like that in the Temple at all.

The tax gatherer keeps his distance from the holy man. He has nothing to say in his own defence. He is a bad lot and he knows it. ' God forgive me! ' is his only prayer, but he offers it with all his heart. And his prayer is heard. He and not the Pharisee is ' justified ' in the sight of God.

Prayer is an expression of character. Words alone do

not make prayer. Jesus could not endure pretentiousness
—and devotional attitudinizing.

4

'Everyone that asketh receiveth'? (11.10). It is a hard
saying. True prayer is the whole strength of the whole man
going out after his desires. A perfunctory passing request
is not prayer. But even if we 'seek', and make our lives
support our prayers, often nothing seems to happen. To
overcome our own indifference of spirit we need to go on
knocking at God's door.

But still there is our experience of disappointment and
baffled desires. The apparently unconditional promise is
startling. Perhaps we do receive, but not precisely what
we asked for: rather something better and more suited to
our real need. Perhaps it is another door that opens than
the one at which we knock, and yet when we enter we know
it is the place where we ought to be.

Jesus never said that His followers could have whatever
they liked. If we knew what it would mean to have some of
our requests granted we should thank God for refusing
them. Some of us, looking back over the years, do so
thank Him. True prayer is seeking God's will not our own:
'Thy will not mine be done.' And nothing better could
possibly happen to us than His will for us.

Augustine's mother prayed that God would not let her
son go to Rome, fearing its temptations. But he went and
it was in Italy that he found Christ. Afterwards he wrote
in his Confessions: 'What was she praying for, O my God,
with all those tears but that You should not allow me to
sail! But You saw deeper and granted the essential of her
prayer. You did not do what she was at that moment asking, that You might do the thing she was always asking.'
(Book 5.8. Translation by F. J. Sheed.)

5

Prayer cannot be the whole of life. To think only and
all the time about God, if that were possible, would make
it impossible for us to serve Him in the tasks He has given
us. On the other hand to concern oneself solely with the

needs of men even with a view to serving them would lead inevitably to superficiality and ineffectiveness. ' But faith can be, and should be, pervasive of all life; for a man may plough the field having perfect trust in God in his heart and yet give his whole attention to driving his furrow straight and turning his corner well. Such a man is truly said to " have God in all his thoughts ". But that faith will fade if he has not his habit of religious practice, his times of prayer and public worship and communion; and in those times he will come to find the focus of all that sustains him in his labour and his human relationships.'[1]

[1] W. Temple, *Thoughts on Some Problems of the Day*, pp. 26f.

V

JESUS THE HEALER

He is a path, if any be misled;
  He is a robe, if any naked be;
If any chance to hunger, He is bread;
  If any be a bondman, He is free;
  If any be but weak, how strong is He!
    To dead men, life is He; to sick men, health;
    To blind men, sight; and to the needy, wealth;
A pleasure without loss; a treasure without stealth.
Giles Fletcher

IN his second volume Luke quotes one of the first Christian sermons describing Jesus as ' a man accredited to you by God through miracles, wonders and signs, which God performed by him among you (as you yourselves know) ' (Acts 2.22 Moffatt). From the outset Jesus was known as a doer of mighty deeds, and not only as a teacher. He healed the sick. He brought sanity to distraught minds. He touched the leper and made friends with the outcast. He forgave sins. It was even said that He commanded the waves and raised the dead.

To the first Christians these events were evidence that the powers of the Kingdom of God were at work in their midst. To many of us to-day, however, such stories present great difficulties. Dogmatic assertions in the name of science that ' miracles do not happen ' have replaced confident appeals to the miracles as proof of the divinity of Christ. What are we to believe?

It is not possible, as some have supposed, to peel off layers of later legendary impositions in order to reach a simple original story without miracles. Miracles are there in the earliest strata of the Gospel tradition. The companions and first disciples of Jesus were persuaded of His possession of extraordinary powers of healing and exorcism. Jesus Himself claimed to possess such powers. The stories of His exercise of them are inextricably mingled with the fabric of the Gospels. It is impossible to remove them without rejecting altogether the credibility of the Gospels as a whole which on other grounds would be an entirely irrational proceeding. Granted that the point of view of the reporters was not that of the modern western world and would inevitably colour the details of the narratives, the main issue cannot be evaded. Miracles are part, an irremovable part, of the Gospel story. At the very least, the fact that His associates believed that He did such things is important testimony to the impression His personality made upon them.

The four Gospels attribute thirty-five particular miracles to Jesus. Even more impressive is the fact that these were selected only as samples of what, so they say, He was doing all the time. The general summaries which occur in all the Gospels are very significant. It is enough for our purposes to refer to those in Luke. After a Sabbath day in Capernaum, ' when the sun was setting, all they that had any sick with divers diseases brought them unto him, and he laid his hands on every one of them and healed them. And devils also came out from many, crying out and saying, " Thou art the Son of God." And rebuking them he suffered them not to speak because they knew that he was the Christ.' (4.40-41; Matt. 8.16-17; Mark 1.32-34.)

Before giving his account of the ' Sermon on the Mount ', Luke says that ' a great number . . . came to hear him and be healed of their diseases; and they that were troubled with unclean spirits were healed. And all the multitude sought to touch him; for power came forth from him and healed them all ' (6.17-19).

When John the Baptist sent to ask Jesus if He was really the Messiah, Luke tells us that He ' cured many of diseases and plagues and evil spirits; and on many that were blind he bestowed sight '. Such deeds as these, He told the messengers, are my credentials (7.18-23; cf. 8.2-3; 10.13; Matt. 4.23; 9.35; Mark 1.39; 3.10-12).

Such passages convey, and are meant to convey, a regular ministry of healing.

It is of course impossible here to discuss the question of miracle at any length, but something must be said. The word itself is ambiguous. *Murray's English Dictionary* defines miracle as ' a marvellous event occurring within human experience, which cannot have been brought about by human power, or by the operation of any natural agency, and must therefore be ascribed to the special intervention of the Deity, or of some supernatural being; chiefly an act (e.g. of healing) exhibiting control over the laws of Nature, and serving as evidence that the agent is either divine or is specially favoured by God.' Let us accept that definition.

The *possibility* of miracle is involved in belief in God: in an atheistic universe there could be no miracles, as there could be no prayer and no purpose in human life. Science accepts as a fundamental postulate the rationality and order of nature. There is no Christian reason for wishing to deny this and many for wishing to assert it. Christianity does not believe in a capricious universe. Jesus believed in an ordered, impartial universe, where rain fell upon the unjust as well as the just. He told us to learn from the regularity of nature. He never encouraged men to think that this order could be upset to suit their convenience. But He taught, to use modern phraseology, that the natural law is the reflection of the Divine will: and so is the supernatural, though we do not yet fully understand its order. The New Testament believes that the supernatural inter-penetrates and influences the natural.

The so-called ' laws of nature ' are formulations of observed sequences of events, so far as human experience and knowledge go. Increasing knowledge of nature may, and often does, lead to a revision of the formulae of generalization. To believe in the orderliness of nature does not involve belief in a closed system of mechanical causation. The human will can initiate and manipulate events without ' breaking the laws '; how much more the divine will, with God's complete understanding of the universe He made. He is constantly at work within the process of His creation, controlling it by the laws inherent in it by His own creative act. ' He follows for the most part the routine that is apparent to us as the uniformity of nature; but there are also occasions when His own constancy requires that in face of special emergencies He should act in an exceptional way; such action will be in a special measure a revelation,'[1] what is commonly called a miracle.

Accordingly, if on other grounds one has come to accept the Christian faith in Jesus as divine, the supreme revela-

[1] Temple, *Christus Veritas*, p. 101.

tion of God, a unique figure in human history, then it is entirely natural and reasonable to believe that unique events and unique powers should be associated with His Person. If He alone among men had unbroken fellowship and unity of purpose with God, He might well have had unique command over nature. Granted Him, who can say what would be normal.

But it cannot be said too clearly that the establishment of the *possibility* of miracle does not necessarily mean the acceptance of every miracle attributed to Him as having happened precisely as the story records it. Each must be taken separately in the light of the evidence. It is not necessary to counter the dogmatic assertions of those who deny that miracles could ever happen by a defence of the literal accuracy of every Gospel story. Even an actual eye-witness may be honestly mistaken. One assertion can be made with confidence. If these stories were deliberate inventions they would have been very different, and more care would have been taken to smooth over the difficulties. They impress by their restraint. Imagination run riot produces such miracles as are to be found in the apocryphal Gospels (see p. 26). And the interesting collections of supposed parallels to the Gospel miracles from Jewish and Hellenistic sources for the most part only demonstrate that they are without parallel.

Yet if deliberate invention must be ruled out, it still remains true that the stories present difficulties. The reporters were not scientifically trained observers and they were not asking scientific questions. Some of the events may not have been miracles at all in the usual sense. Was the daughter of Jairus really dead? If we take the words of Jesus literally, she was not. The stilling of the storm may have been a coincidence, for storms on the Lake come and go with astonishing rapidity. It has been suggested that the feeding of the five thousand was a miracle of fellowship rather than a miracle of multiplication. Jesus set the example of sharing and the crowd followed suit, so that there proved to be enough for all. Was the ' miraculous ' draught of fish the result of Jesus detecting signs of the presence of a shoal which had escaped the practised eyes of the fishermen? It is not difficult to suggest such and similar ' rationalizations ' for some of the stories, and there is nothing to be ashamed of in trying to understand exactly what happened. But even if such guesses be true, it is impossible thus to explain away the record. And there still remains the overwhelming impression made upon the observers by the Person of Jesus. We may have to say frankly that we do not know what happened, any more than the observers did. We may feel that a modern witness might have reported the event differently. But those who were there believed that a signal action of God had taken place. Making all allowance for possible misunderstanding and exaggeration there is overwhelming evidence that Jesus did work miracles.

Luke as a doctor was naturally specially interested in the stories of Jesus as a healer, and collected some from sources of his own which do not appear in the other Gospels. He has five miracle stories of his own to tell.

In the first century many diseases were attributed to the influence of evil spirits. It is not surprising therefore to find that many of the cures wrought by Jesus are described in terms of exorcism, or the driving out of demons from the patients. Whether or not we can categorically deny the possibility of possession by evil spirits, it is at least certain that we should to-day describe these diseases in other terms. Some of the cases show the symptoms of various forms of insanity, or of epilepsy. Among the others recorded are such troubles as blindness, deafness and dumbness (11.14) which might have been due, as we say, to 'nervous' and mental causes, like 'shell shock'. Assuming that modern science is correct, many people are troubled by these stories, because Jesus certainly speaks and acts as if He shared the common belief of His time. It is possible that He was accommodating Himself to the beliefs of the patients, humouring them in order to establish a basis for a cure. Even modern doctors have been known to do that! If He had spoken in terms of the still imperfect science of this or any preceding generation He would have been unintelligible. It seems much more likely however that Jesus shared the belief of His contemporaries in scientific matters, just as no doubt He accepted without question their views as to the authorship of the scriptures. The possession of infallible knowledge would have made it impossible for Him to share the life of man as surely as if He had never known hunger and fatigue. To suggest otherwise is to cast doubt on the reality of His humanity. However this may be, the power of Jesus over these wretched beings is one of the best attested features of the Gospel portrait.

While it is not always possible, in the absence of a scientific diagnosis, to discuss the Gospel cases in the light of modern medical knowledge, it seems that many were similar to those often treated successfully to-day by 'suggestion'. Mental and spiritual causes lie behind many diseases and the removal of them is involved in the cure. Much has been, and is still being, learned about the relations of 'soul' and 'body'. While it would be very misleading to describe the Gospel miracles as instances of 'faith healing' in the modern sense, yet faith in this connection does seem to be used as equivalent to trust in the power and willingness of Jesus, or of God working through Jesus, to perform a cure. In several of the stories Jesus seems to be taking pains to establish this relationship of confidence. In others the faith is there already. 'Faith' has not here the theological meaning that it has acquired in the epistles or in some other parts of the Gospels. In the miracle stories the word cannot usually stand for belief in any doctrine about Jesus as Messiah or Son of God.[1]

Yet even if light is thrown upon some of the cures of Jesus by our growing knowledge of the laws of mind and spirit, it does not really help us to dismiss, if we wish to dismiss, the idea of miracle. Nothing we know now explains them all and it still remains a marvel that He did them then and in that way. He understood two thousand years ago laws which we are only now beginning to master after generations of research. He performed, often instantaneously, cures that demand even to-day prolonged treatment and complicated apparatus. Even supposing the widow's son at Nain (7.11-17) was in a coma and not dead, who was this who could recognize the condition at a glance and effect an immediate restoration? It is certainly inter-

[1] e.g. in 5.20 faith means confidence on the part of the bearers, and presumably also the sick man, that Jesus would and could do what they wanted. So in 7.9 the faith of the centurion so warmly commended by Jesus was a complete trust in His power to heal. Cf. also 8.48; 18.42. In the majority of the stories in Luke no reference is made to the faith of the sick person.

esting to compare modern cases with those in the Gospels, but it does not lessen the marvel.

Some reference has already been made to the so-called 'nature miracles'. Here especially we cannot feel sure that we know what happened as it might have appeared to a modern witness. We need not be ashamed of trying to understand precisely what took place, or of saying frankly that we do not know. And when all is said there remains the impression made by Jesus which caused the story to be recorded at all. For example, the great haul of fish, whatever its cause, amazed the fishermen (5.1-11). No doubt the story of how Jesus called His disciples from their nets to be fishers of men is recorded because as they thought it over afterwards they saw in its details symbolic significance. Something tremendous happened to Peter which turned him from the old trade to the new. He saw Jesus and himself with new eyes. If a miracle be an event which brings a special revelation of God, this was a miracle, however the fish were caught.

But the fact that we find these stories more difficult to understand than the healing miracles does not prove that they are not true. Again it goes back to our judgment about Jesus. If we believe in His divinity, the 'laws' of gravitation are no more and no less obstacles to His power than those of anatomy or physiology. The question still remains as to precisely what He did do on those occasions, but not the question whether He *could* have done what the onlookers apparently thought He did.

Why did Jesus work miracles? The Gospels give us less direct light on this than we might have expected. In nearly all the healing stories recorded by Luke nothing is said about the motive of Jesus. But when He brought back to life the widow's son at Nain, it is definitely said that He was moved by compassion for the mother (7.11-17), and when He cured the woman with curvature of the spine (13.11-17) and the man with dropsy (14.1-6) He compared the deeds to the works of mercy which were exempt from the Sabbath law. On every page of the Gospel is apparent the deep sympathy of Jesus for men and women, with their wrecked lives, their physical and mental sufferings, their heartrending sorrows, the tragedy of their sins. Not less apparent is His determination to right their lot. What a joy it must have been to Him to declare in such a world the love of the Father in heaven, even to the unthankful and the evil! What a joy to act with power as the Father's emancipating agent!

He emphatically asserted of all such deeds that they were evidence of the presence of the Kingdom of God, of the irruption into this world of a new manifestation of the creative power of God. He told the messengers from John the Baptist that they were sufficient proof that He was the looked-for Messiah (7.19-23). On another occasion He told His critics: ' If I with the finger of God cast out devils, no doubt the Kingdom of God is come upon you.' God in Him was waging war upon Satan (11.14-22). In some sense the miracles were His credentials.

Yet in His story of the Temptation He told of His decision not to rely upon wonders to coerce the minds of men. And more than once He ordered those whom He had cured to tell nobody, which again is evidence that He did not do these works in order to win man's allegiance (8.56; 5.14).

This work of healing was no side issue. It was an essential part of His mission. This was the Gospel in action. It was His vocation both to preach and to heal, and it was to that double task that He called His followers (9.1-6; 10.9). He thought of disease as an intruder in God's world. When His disciples reported their own successes in healing He rejoiced in it as evidence that Satan's rule was broken (10.18; cf. 11.20).

The Christian Church has never forgotten this double commission. In Britain nowadays hospitals and medical work are not, for the most part, conducted under the direct auspices of the Church; but they were originally. We owe our hospitals to Christ. Now the community as a whole has taken over this work from the Church, as it has many other forms of social and educational work. In nearly all countries of the world medical pioneering has been done by Christian societies and in many countries a large part is still in their hands. Whatever the auspices, no class in the community is doing a more Christ-like work than doctors and nurses. And the growing recognition by the medical profession of the close inter-relation of ' body ' and ' soul ' and of the importance of ' spiritual healing ' is opening up renewed possibilities of fruitful collaboration with Christian ministers.

E

It is, however, needful to remind some people that indiscriminate assurances about the healing power of faith and prayer are dangerous and are not warranted by the Gospels. Death comes to every man in the providence of God. Cure is not always accessible to faith. The prayer of Jesus in Gethsemane here, as always, is our model; and to Him then the answer came not in relief from suffering but in strength to go through it.

The whole matter is well summed up by Dr. Lewis in the *Abingdon Commentary* (p. 929): ' If one sees in Jesus Christ simply a Galilean peasant of unusual religious insight, then one will naturally question the accounts of his miraculous deeds, except perhaps a few of the healings. It will be useless for those who accept this view of Christ to plead that they reject the miracles because of the inadequacy of the evidence—which was Hume's position. It is *the thing itself* and not the evidence which is the real stumbling-block of the sceptic. Miracles simply " do not happen " and that settles it. But if miracles do not happen then there could not be such a person as Christ is represented to be, for he is himself the supreme miracle beside which the greatest of his works appears as insignificant. The Christ of the New Testament cannot be explained on a purely naturalistic basis without doing violence not alone to the records but to historical Christian experience. Admit *him* and the works ascribed to him take on verisimilitude for they are just the kind of works that such a person may be expected to accomplish. . . . If in Jesus Christ God made a manifestation of himself such as he has made nowhere else, then we may expect uniqueness of action to go with the uniqueness of personality.'

VI

JESUS AND
THE SOCIAL ORDER

Give us hearts of flame,
To burn against the cold
To burn against the old, the mortal chill
The quenching thrill
Of the fast-flooding tide.
Thou art Fire and Light
(Give us hearts of flame!)
Make us to burn like beacons
In defiance of ancient Night
Make us braziers in the cold streets of the cities,
Make us lamps in Thy sanctuaries,
Make us candles to the Sacred Heart,
The world is lost, and is looking for the way.

M. Farrow

'MASTER, bid my brother divide the inheritance with me,' cried someone to Jesus. 'But he said unto him, Man, who made me a judge or a divider over you? And he said unto them, Take heed and keep yourselves from all covetousness: for a man's life consisteth not in the abundance of the things which he possesseth' (12.13-15).

On another occasion (20.19-26) some Pharisees demanded to know if He was in favour of paying taxes to Rome. If he said 'no', He would get into trouble with the authorities. If He said 'yes', He would alienate the sympathies of the people. Either way the questioners stood to gain. 'Give to Caesar what belongs to Caesar,' replied Jesus, 'and give to God what belongs to God.' Caesar had his rights. There were imperial services from which they all profited and for which a return was reasonable. By implication Jesus disowned rebellion against Rome, as He did at other times. He saw only too clearly where that road led—to suffering, death and destruction. But God had His rights too. (Was Jesus thinking of Genesis 1.27? The coins had

Caesar's image. Man was stamped with God's image, however defaced and blurred.) Let His questioners make sure
they were rendering them. That was the supreme issue.

These two incidents illustrate the teaching of Jesus about
'social questions'. He was not a social reformer and
advanced no programme of reform. He would not be a
judge or an arbitrator in political or social disputes. Not
only were our modern social and economic problems beyond the horizon of the Gospels, so also in a sense were
the social and economic problems of their own time. When
such questions came before Jesus He lifted them on to a
different plane. The Kingdom of God is not a religious
name for Utopia. Does this mean that we look to Him in
vain for light in this realm? By no means.

It is plausibly argued by some people that the social conditions of the time of Jesus were so completely different
from ours that nothing He said about them could possibly
have any bearing upon our large-scale complexities. That
would no doubt be true if Jesus had in fact legislated about
social questions. Others, much less plausibly, assert that
Jesus in any case expected the end of the world within a
generation and that His teaching was intended only for the
guidance of life under the threat of dissolution—an ' interim
ethic '. Without going here into the larger issue which we
have already discussed (pp. 41ff.) it can at least be said that
the actual teaching of Jesus appears rather to assume the
continuance of normal living. A true ' interim ethic ' would
urge, as Paul did, that the time was short and that earthly
affairs mattered little. ' They that have wives (should) be
as though they had none; and they that weep as though they
wept not; and they that rejoice as though they rejoiced not;
and they that buy as though they possessed not; and they
that use this world as not abusing it: for the fashion of
this world passeth away ' (1 Cor. 7.29-31). Jesus Himself
appealed to timeless principles based upon the nature of
God and the proper life for His children (see p. 71).

At the other extreme are those who mistakenly think that
loyalty to Jesus demands the attempt to lift His sayings
from their context in the life of His time and apply them
as rules for literal observance to-day. But to take Jesus
seriously is not the same thing as to take Him literally. As
Karl Barth has said of such literalism, this ethic ' is not

applicable to the problems of contemporary society nor yet to any conceivable society '. (On this see pp. 115f.)

1

The foundation of the concern of Jesus—and of the Christian—for the social order is the fact that God is our Father. The Kingdom of God, we have said, is not a religious name for Utopia. But just because it means the sovereignty of God over freely surrendered human personalities, and because it reveals the true relation of men to their Creator-Father and to one another, its coming is more fundamental to social welfare than any scheme of social planning could possibly be. If God rules in a man's heart he will do what lies in him to make His will done in community life. ' Be the sons of your Father,' said Jesus. Realize your true nature and find your true freedom in obedience to His will.

For our fellows too are God's children. We do not know the meaning of life until we realize this. Men are immortal souls made in God's image, however marred by sin. Every human being is different, of value to God for his own sake and with a unique life to live. He matters. God loves him. We shall not know how to order society until we see it in the light of God's purpose for the world He made and His plan for human life. Only if man is seen in his true stature as more than the citizen of any earthly state can we learn the secret of true citizenship here upon earth. What is the world here for anyway? What is man? Is there a purpose in human life? If so, have we any clue to its nature? These are really the fundamental questions for politics and economics no less than for religion and philosophy, because upon the answer men give to them will depend the nature of the state and the nature of the social order.

The religious life as Jesus presented it is not a life of solitary contemplation and withdrawal. There is a second commandment like unto the first (10.27). The new life in God expresses itself in love of one's neighbour.

> What life have you if you have not life together?
> There is no life that is not in community,
> And no community not lived in praise of God.[1]

[1] T. S. Eliot.

Man comes into life as a member of society. He lives, grows, learns, through society and its groupings. The value of his education by the community will be shown so far as he comes to have ' a mind of his own ' with which to criticize and contribute. He receives and gives at every point, or ought to. It is unreal to isolate men and community or to set them in opposition. Jesus steadily held them together.

' Creation,' says Martin Buber, ' is not a hurdle on the road to God, it is the road itself. We are created along with one another and directed to a life with one another. Creatures are placed in my way so that I, their fellow creature, by means of them and with them find the way to God.'[1]

In nothing is modern man more in danger of losing the worth of his human and Christian heritage than in the tendency to lose his sense of community. Mr. Eliot's picture needs qualification, but it is all too true of modern man that he lives

> . . . dispersed on ribbon roads,
> And no man knows or cares who is his neighbour
> Unless his neighbour makes too much disturbance,
> But all dash to and fro in motor cars,
> Familiar with the roads and settled nowhere.
> Nor does the family ever move about together,
> But every son would have his motor cycle,
> And daughters ride away on casual pillions.

The theological implications of the Kingdom of God are discussed elsewhere and they must not be forgotten. But it is clear that Jesus meant those who accepted the sovereignty of God over their lives to practise in community the laws of the Kingdom, to express its spirit in all their relationships. They were to be a distinctive group with a flavour to them, like salt. They were to stand out in darkness like a light; to be obvious to everyone like a city on a hill. They were to embody life as God meant it to be.

2

The Father's care is not for man's spiritual welfare alone. He knows that men need clothes, food and drink. He

[1] *Between Man and Man*, p. 52.

provides for all. It is not His will if the rapacity and greed of some prevent all from having their due share. If we seek the Kingdom of God, the rule of the Father, in daily life, all these things will be added to us: there will be enough for all (12.22-34).

There is no trace in the teaching or life of Jesus of the ascetic philosophy which holds that material goods and pleasures are evil in themselves. They may be misused but they are gifts of God for our enjoyment. The Son of Man came eating and drinking (7.34). Food, clothing, home and family life, the beauty of nature, social fellowship, are all in the purpose of God and may be used in His service. The occasion may arise when for the sake of the Kingdom home and possessions, parents and friends, bodily health or life itself must be given up. But He never teaches abstention for its own sake, or suspicion of pleasure because it is pleasure.

Man is a meeting place of spiritual, material and social factors. His biographer said of Plotinus that he was ashamed that his soul lived in his body. There have been religions, and even forms of Christianity, which held that moral and religious problems would be solved in proportion as the soul became detached from the body. True Christianity has a healthy streak of materialism in it. It recognizes that men are not disembodied spirits. No man, it has been said, can be a hero, a lover or a poet unless he has recently had something to eat. A true ethic must deal with real men and women, made up of this baffling, exciting and sometimes irritating amalgam of soul and body. Your Father, said Jesus, knows that you need food and clothes (12.30).

For Jesus the whole world was His Father's family. His affection for ordinary folk, peasant, fishers, artisans, is obvious from the Gospel stories, as is His special sympathy for the suffering and the handicapped, the submerged and the oppressed: even for 'quisling' publicans and for Samaritans. (4.18; 7.22; 14.13; 16.19-31; 5.27; 7.36-50; 19.7.) And He made it clear by both His actions and His words that He knew that in this as in all else He was revealing the mind of His Father (15.7 and 10). All that breaks the family unity is abhorrent to Him; the acquisitive spirit, that tries to grab more than its share at the family table; political or ecclesiastical arrogance; the indifference of the

haves to the have-nots. Love one another, even your
enemies, if you want to be like your Father in heaven, He
said. And by love He meant something costly and practical,
not mere amiable feelings or vague goodwill.

3

Jesus did not wish to abolish leadership and authority,
but He had a new test for greatness. As things were, rank
was secured and held by self-assertion. In the Kingdom of
God the mark of rank was to be self-sacrifice and service.
The 'great' were no more important in the sight of God
than 'the least of these, my brethren' (Matt. 25.40). No
man had any right to exploit another for his own pleasure
or profit. Ability and ambition were to be yoked for service. 'The kings of the Gentiles rule over them and their
authorities take the name of Benefactor: not so with you.
He who is greatest among you must be like the youngest,
and he who is chief like a servant. Which is the greatest,
guest or servant? Is it not the guest? But I am among
you as a servant' (22.25-27 Moffatt).

To create a Christ-like social order demands more than
goodwill, more than love, even in Christ's sense of the word.
Cool heads are needed as much as warm hearts: hard work
and inventiveness and planning to overcome the recalcitrant
practical problems. It is nonsense to say that if we were all
Christians there would be no social problems. But if the
practical men and women were animated by the spirit of
Christ and lived in the light of these Christian principles—
there seems no other word—there would be a chance of
solving the world's stubborn social and international problems. And not otherwise (6.47-49).

The teaching of Jesus on social questions is thus occasional rather than systematic and must be drawn out by
inference. There are, however, two subjects to which He
makes direct and explicit reference, the family and the use
of money. His teaching about sex and family relations
is considered in the next chapter. His teaching about the
use of money is surprisingly full and most revealing of His
outlook on social life, and may be conveniently examined
now.

At first sight it looks as if the statement made above,

about the attitude of Jesus to material goods, did not fit the facts. For we find that Luke contains a number of passages, peculiar to his Gospel, hostile to wealth and its possession. The Magnificat sets the tone: 'The hungry he hath filled with good things and the rich he hath sent empty away' (1.53). At Nazareth Jesus applies to Himself the passage from Isaiah 61: 'The Lord . . . anointed me to preach good tidings to the poor' (4.18; cf. 7.22). Luke alone reports the woes upon the rich: 'Woe unto you that are rich, for ye have received your consolation. Woe unto you, ye that are full now, for ye shall hunger' (6.25f.). He alone gives us the stern story of the foolish rich man who laid up treasure for himself but was not rich towards God (12.13-21). Here alone is told the story of the Rich Man and the Beggar (16.19-31). In his Gospel alone is found the unqualified assertion: 'So therefore whosoever he be of you that renounceth not all that he hath, he cannot be my disciple' (14.33). Even in sayings drawn from Q, Luke's version often adds a sting that is absent from Matthew's. Matthew tells us that Jesus said: 'Blessed are the poor in spirit.' Luke renders it: 'Blessed are ye poor,' apparently changing the emphasis from a spiritual condition to a material (Matt. 5.3; Luke 6.20). When both record the exhortation not to lay up treasures on earth, Luke adds: 'Sell that ye have and give alms' (Matt. 6.19-21; Luke 12.33). On such grounds Luke is often held to teach that wealth in itself is evil and that poverty in itself is a passport to the Kingdom. It is alleged that Dives was tormented because he was rich, and that Lazarus went to Abraham's bosom because he was a beggar.

Closer attention, however, makes it clear that such an interpretation of Luke's attitude, or to express it better, of the teaching of Jesus as reported by Luke, would be very superficial. For one thing, there are also passages in Luke's Gospel which run counter to any alleged antagonism to the rich. If Dives is not allowed into paradise, yet wealthy Abraham is there as well as beggar Lazarus. Luke alone records that the work of Jesus was in part at least financed by the wealth of a group of women (8.2-3). He tells us of the praise of Jesus for the rich publican of Jericho, though he apparently kept a good proportion of his wealth (19.1-10). He speaks with respect and approval of the wealthy Joseph of Arimathea (23.50-53). He alone tells us how Jesus spoke of the profitable use to which ' the mammon of unrighteousness ' might be put, in making friends.

The shorter version of the first Beatitude given by Luke, ' Blessed are ye poor,' is thought by most scholars to represent the words actually spoken by Jesus. Nevertheless the meaning of them is more accurately conveyed to the modern reader by Matthew in ' Blessed are the poor in spirit '. For the word ' poor ' had special associations in Judaism in the time of Jesus. His hearers would understand it to mean the faithful and God-fearing rather than the people with very little money. Already in the later Old Testament writings ' poverty ' had acquired religious associations (e.g. Isa. 66.2). By New Testament times ' poverty ' implied not only social status but even more the religious attitude of humility and receptiveness. The saying certainly cannot be taken as meaning that Jesus taught that poverty in our modern sense of the word is a blessing. Only once was the surrender of all possessions made a condition of discipleship and that was apparently an exceptional case demanding exceptional treatment (18.18-27).

Yet this very story of the ' ruler ', i.e. probably an official of the local synagogue, reveals the unmistakable sternness in the teaching of Jesus about wealth. The tendency of most of us to soften His uncompromising words to ease their pressure on our consciences is just one more illustration of that ' deceitfulness of riches ' (Mark 4.19) upon which He insisted. We are all apt to confuse what we have with what we are (12.15). In His sad comment on the ruler's refusal Jesus did not say that it was difficult for a rich man to get into the Kingdom of God. He said it was impossible, except by a miracle, so great is the handicap of wealth. ' The rich man,' wrote Dr. Cadoux, ' used to finding in his wealth the key to all doors, stands before the door of the Kingdom of God as helplessly absurd as a camel contemplating the passage of a needle's eye.'

And it is no sound exegesis that tries to turn the camel into a cable (Greek KAMELOS into KAMILOS), or the needle's eye into a side gate through which, by going down on its knees, the camel might wriggle its way! Jesus was quoting a proverb for the impossible, which is to be found in slightly different form in the Talmud and the Koran. Like the disciples we may be exceedingly amazed at such a reversal of currently accepted standards and feel that in fact it is easier for the rich to be religious than for the poor, but there is no doubt as to what Jesus said.

Jesus actually emphasized the perils of the acquisitive instinct more than the evils of drunkenness or sexual vice. Covetousness absorbs and petrifies the spirit. It darkens the inner eye. It makes a man think, like the Rich Fool, of ' my goods ' instead of ' our daily bread '. Wealth gives men an illusory sense of security and satisfaction. The sudden summons of death to the Rich Fool is not recorded as a judgment. The point is rather that the goods on which he prided himself had suddenly become valueless, and he had no other riches left to take with him into the presence of God. He had been too busy to acquire them (12.16-21).

The sternest of all Christ's parables deals with the same theme (16.19-31). In the story of Dives and Lazarus is revealed what Dale called ' the indignation of infinite love at white heat '. To Jesus such a life as that of Dives, highly respectable and ordinary as it was, is profoundly immoral. It is sometimes complained that Dives did nothing for which he could be blamed. That is just the point. Dives was condemned precisely because he did nothing. He accepted the existing order of society without effort and without protest, because it suited him. A wealthy man has a beggar at his gate, and nothing is done. Such selfish living is a deadly sin. Here is a man of privilege who is unfit to have it.

Is the parable then an attack on the wealthy and a defence of the poor? Is Jesus an advocate of the class struggle? It can hardly be a condemnation of all rich men or Abraham would not be presiding at the feast. Yet does it not suggest that such extremes of poverty and wealth as Lazarus and Dives represent are in themselves unjustifiable? Can we make any protest if heaven reverses the situation and fills the hungry with good things while it sends the rich empty away? Doubtless the fine linen and champagne of Dives were as little deserved as the rags of Lazarus. ' You've had your turn, Dives. Now it is the turn of Lazarus.'

But, of course, Jesus was probing deeper than that. Selfish wealth while abject poverty exists is itself an evil. It denies brotherhood. It corrupts the souls of rich and

poor alike. It digs a gulf between men (cf. 16.26). On earth
Dives had carefully insulated himself from Lazarus. Even
if he had tried to make friends, the difference in their positions would have made real friendship impossible. Even
well-used wealth digs a gulf.

Dives just took the social order for granted. He was
probably not specially inhuman. He was callous about the
needs he saw every day, but it probably never occurred to
him that they were any responsibility of his. He didn't
really *see* Lazarus. He just took him for granted as part of
the street scene. To be wealthier than one's fellows, as
John Bennett has put it, ' blinds one to the need of change
and makes one's mind a nest of rationalizations in defence
of one's own privilege '.

The sting of the parable is in its reference to the five
brothers, living as Dives had lived and in peril of a like end.
Who were the brothers? Surely just those to whom Jesus
was speaking; and perhaps you and me.

It is often said, or used to be, that what Jesus called for
was ' the stewardship of our possessions '. Unfortunately
that has too often been taken to cover only the disposal of
the surplus, instead of the whole of life, the earning of
money no less than the spending of it. Even the greatest
generosity on the part of individual rich men, admirable as
it may be in itself, is no justification for extremes of wealth
and poverty. It is very hard to acquire great wealth without injustice to others. It is hard to be rich, and to live
with others on a level of common humanity. It is hard to
give wealth away without doing harm. The charity of the
wealthy is often dictatorship rather than stewardship.

Jesus did commend alms-giving (6.30; 12.33), probably
in His day the best available way of helping those in need,
though He warned men that even giving may be robbed of
any spiritual value if it be done for motives of ostentation
(Matt. 6.2-4). The aim of giving must be service and sympathy must go with it. A service rendered in expectation
of a return gift (14.12-14) is no giving. There are limits to
what charity can do, but Dives might have done much for
Lazarus. His sores might have been attended to: he might
have been given a square meal and enabled to start life
again. In the hands of the good Samaritan, money can
help to rescue the robber's victim (10.30-37). It can pro-

vide hospitality for the unfortunate (14.12-14). However far the State goes in taking over care for health and social security and in abolishing extremes of wealth and poverty, there will always be room for the Christian 'extra' of human kindliness, and the giving of money will no doubt always have its part to play.

It is beyond the scope of this book to discuss in detail what the Christian use of money means in the modern world.[1] But it may safely be said that there is no point at which the sincerity of our Christian professions is more tested than in our attitude to money. The whole teaching of Jesus about the social order comes to a focus here.

The unforgivable sin, the sin of Dives, is complacency. 'Christ taught us to care,' wrote von Hügel. 'Caring is the great thing. Caring matters most.'

---

[1] I may perhaps be allowed to say that I did once try to work this out in a book called *Christ and Money,* now out of print.

VII

JESUS AND THE FAMILY

*I bow my knee unto the Father, from whom
every family in heaven and on earth is named.*
St. Paul

'I WILL now speak on the behalf of women, to take away
their reproach. For as death and the curse came into
the world by a woman, so also did life and healtth: God
sent forth His Son, made of a woman . . . When the
Saviour was come, woman rejoiced in Him, before either
man or angel. I read not that ever any man did give unto
Christ so much as one groat; but the women followed Him,
and ministered to Him of their substance. 'Twas a woman
that washed His feet with tears, and a woman that anointed
His body to the burial. They were women that wept when
He was going to the cross and women that followed Him
from the cross, and that sat by His sepulchre, when He was
buried. They were women that were first with Him at His
resurrection-morn, and women that brought tidings first to
His disciples that He was risen from the dead. Women
therefore are highly favoured, and show by these things
that they are sharers with us in the grace of life.'

So John Bunyan, through the mouth of Gaius, in his
Pilgrim's Progress. ' Sharers with men in the grace of life '
—that is the revolutionary doctrine of Christianity. It
changed the position of woman in the ancient world and
gave her a status unknown in Greece or Rome. And
wherever Christianity has gone it has brought a new idea
of womanhood and transformed her place in society. Professor Gilbert Murray has written that ' the special appeal
which it made to women '[1] was one of the reasons for the
spread of Christianity in its early days. Those who are
most forward in quoting from St. Paul's Letter to the Corinthians the rules he lays down to meet temporary and

[1] *Four Stages of Greek Religion*, p. 179.

local conditions as expressing his attitude to women, sometimes forget his bold assertion, 'there is neither male nor female, for ye are all one in Christ Jesus' (Gal. 3.28). However it may have been with the apostle, there is no question that his Lord broke away from current teachings and conventions. It was surprising for a rabbi to be found talking with a woman, but He gave of His best to the woman of Samaria (John 4.27). He accepted the gifts and personal service of women in the support of His ministry (8.1-3). He numbered Mary and Martha among His closest friends. He welcomed women into the Kingdom on the same terms as men. He set them on a level before God.

All this to our generation is apt to seem the most obvious of commonplaces. We have forgotten already the long struggle for the dignity and freedom of womanhood and the achievements of even the last hundred years. We still do not take the issue as seriously as it deserves.

At least in His own day the teaching of Jesus about the relations of men and women was revolutionary. Mithraism, the most popular rival of Christianity in its early generations, was like Islam, a religion for men; and so in some measure was Judaism. This is not to suggest that the Jews did not have high standards of sex relations. Family loyalty was part of the loyalty demanded by Jehovah. Monogamy was the practice, though the letter of the law allowed polygamy. Women of outstanding ability could hold positions of great influence. Though concubines had a recognized status, prostitution was sternly condemned. Family life reached a general level far above that known elsewhere in the ancient world. And yet woman occupied a secondary and subordinate place. The old idea of woman as property still lingered. In the synagogue the men thanked God that they were not born as women; though there is no indication that the women were similarly encouraged to give thanks for their sex.

The record of the Christian Church in this matter is very mixed. Here, as in so many other issues, it took a long time for Christians fully to understand the implications of Christ's teaching. The bonds of conservatism and convention were hard to break. Even to-day nearly all sections of the Church deny to women positions of authority and responsibility commensurate with their ability and their devotion to its service; to say nothing of the fundamental spiritual equality taught by Christ. Yet when all allowance has been made it is true that the Spirit of Christ has been the great emancipator of woman. The Church has moved regrettably slowly, but it has been throughout the world the pioneer in the education of women and girls and in striving towards equal rights for men and women in society and family life.

1

Our present concern is with the teaching and practice of Jesus who stands here—as everywhere—unchallengeably above the religious leaders and teachers of mankind. Luke's has been called the Gospel of womanhood and it is to him that we owe most of our knowledge of the teaching of Jesus on this subject.

It was pointed out in chapter 2 that the stories of the infancy are told in Luke from the woman's point of view and there are a number of other evidences in the Gospel which suggest that he is indebted to women for his information. Much of what we know about Mary, the mother of Jesus, is told us by him. Luke alone tells us about Elizabeth, the mother of John the Baptist (1.24ff.) and Anna, the aged prophetess who welcomed the baby Jesus in the Temple (2.36). He alone records in the first sermon at Nazareth the reference to the visit of Elijah to the widow of Sidon (4.26). From Luke's Gospel comes the moving story of the restoration of the only son to his widowed mother at Nain (7.11-17). He alone records the anointing by the prostitute in the Pharisee's house (7.36-50). (Not to be confused with the quite different story in Mark 14.3-9; Matt. 26.6-13.) It is from Luke alone that we get particulars about the women who shared the missionary journey with Jesus and the twelve and contributed to their support —though Matthew makes a passing reference to the fact (8.1-3; cf. Matt. 27.55). The mention of the names suggests that they were well known in the Church, and perhaps known personally to Luke himself.

John's Gospel tells us much about the household at Bethany where Jesus was a welcome guest (John 11-12.11), but it is to Luke that we owe the revealing story of Martha's housewifely concern about the dinner while Mary is absorbed in conversation with the guest (10.38-42). Only Luke tells us of the woman in the crowd who called out a blessing upon the mother of Jesus and His reply (11.27-28). From him comes the story of the healing of the woman with spinal weakness, the daughter of Abraham for whose healing the Sabbath was a most fitting day (13.10-17). The woman who rejoiced at the finding of her lost piece of silver is in a parable recorded only by Luke (15.8-10). So is the widow whose importunity forced justice from the indifferent judge (18.1-8). Luke is the only evangelist to record that Jesus bade men 'remember Lot's wife' (17.32). The pity of the daughters of Jerusalem for Jesus as He approached the Cross is only in this Gospel (23.27-31). How much poorer we should be without these stories, and how much they add to our portrait of Jesus.

They are, of course, in addition to a number of incidents which Luke included from Mark or Q (see p. 13). One is the story of how His mother and His brothers wished, as it seems, to protect Jesus from the dangers and strains of His mission. (8.19-21; cf. Mark 3.32-35. 'Friends' here should probably read 'family' or 'relations'.) It is not said, though the passage is often so interpreted, that He refused to see them, nor do His words even imply a censure. But He did declare that the claims of God's service were superior even to those of family ties. Another story which Luke shares with Mark tells of the lesson about giving which Jesus drew from the devotion and sacrifice of a poor widow (21.1-4). All the Gospels tell us that in the closing scenes of Jesus' life almost the only friends who stood by him were women. 'Many women', according to Matthew, watched the crucifixion with tortured hearts 'from afar' (Matt. 27.55-56; Mark 15.40; Luke 23.49). The Fourth Gospel tells us that a smaller group went closer and stood by the Cross—four women and one man (John 19.25-27). Several women followed the body and watched it being laid in the tomb; Joseph of Arimathea is the only man who is named (23.55; Matt. 27.61; Mark 15.47). They went home and prepared spices and ointments for the body, and 'at early dawn', at the first possible moment after the Sabbath, they came to the tomb to perform the last offices. And it was to these women that the stupendous news of

F

the Resurrection was first announced, and they who carried the message to the eleven and the other disciples (23.56-24.12; Matt. 28.1-10; Mark 16.1-8).

It is clear that women take a large place in the Gospel story, loving much because He did much for them, serving Him with selfless devotion; from the day Mary wrapped Him in swaddling clothes and laid Him in the manger, until the day when they went, as they thought, to dress His body for its last rest.

Many scholars believe that the story of the woman taken in adultery, printed in our Authorized Version as John 7.53-8.11 really belongs to Luke. The manuscripts which omit the passage from John are earlier and more numerous than those which include it. The style and vocabulary are not those of the Fourth Gospel. On the other hand, not only would the story find a natural home in Luke's Gospel but the language as carefully analysed by scholars is peculiarly characteristic of Luke. Further an important group of manuscripts actually include the passage in Luke at the end of chapter 21. So it can be concluded from both external and internal evidence that there are, if not decisive, at least very strong reasons for believing that Luke wrote the story and that it belongs to his Gospel.

2

The attitude of Jesus to children is no less noteworthy than His attitude to women. Students of classical literature tell us that it is very hard to find any kind of parallel. The Gospels reflect Jesus' love of children and their own delight in His company. He watched their games with friendly amusement, and once told His audience that grown-up though they might be they were behaving just like children who spoil the game by squabbling. They would follow the lead neither of John nor of Himself (7.31-35). The story of the healing of Jairus' daughter of twelve is marked by a special tenderness. 'Get up, little girl' is His way of recalling the child's spirit to consciousness; just like her mother calling her in the morning. Luke notes with a doctor's approval the insistence that in their joy they must not forget that the child needed food (8.40-56).

The exact meaning of the incident where Jesus took a

child and set him in the midst of the disputing disciples is
not altogether easy to determine (9.46-48). They were
arguing about their respective ranks in the Kingdom. Jesus
took a little child in His arms (in Mark's phrase). ' Don't
be concerned about who the great people are. Be kind to
a little child like this. He is important to me. Don't think
about ambition. Think rather about service, about helping
people who need you—like this child.' So perhaps we may
paraphrase His words. The saying about causing little ones
to stumble (17.1-2) is associated with this incident by
Matthew and Mark, which may well be its original setting.
So placed it is a stern warning to those who contaminate the
innocence of childhood.

One of the most familiar of all Gospel stories tells of the
mothers bringing their children to be blessed by Jesus (18.
15-17). The disciples did not want their Master's time to be
wasted by such a triviality. He was concerned with great
issues about the Kingdom of God; what had children to do
with them? Everything, said Jesus; indeed only those who
come to the Kingdom with trust and receptiveness like theirs
really belong to it. ' Let them come,' said Jesus. They
would come of their own accord if they were not prevented.
That surely tells us something about Jesus. Children liked
to be with Him.

3

It is an impressive fact, moreover, that Jesus used illustrations drawn from the home for His profoundest teaching.
He told us that the nature of the creator and sustainer of
the universe was more like the loving heart of a father than
anything else we could imagine. If men wanted to know
what God was like they were to think of the best possible
human fatherhood; and then believe that God is infinitely
better still. Fatherhood, according to Jesus, is our best
clue to the character of God. He tells us, too, that the
Kingdom of God, the community over which God rules in
reality, will be a great family of men and women living as
brothers and sisters worthily of their Father. So that in the
thought of Jesus the home is woven into the eternal structure
of the universe. All that tells us much about how Jesus
regarded the family.

Yet no systematic teaching about the family is to be found in the New Testament. There is no laying down of a body of regulations about marriage for universal application. Just because marriage was held in such high esteem in Judaism our Lord had no need to say much directly about it. His attitude comes out indirectly, in His personal dealings with women and children, and directly in His reply to a challenge on the question of divorce.

In Mark 10.2-12 (Matt. 19.3-12) He was asked to give His ruling in the current debate between the school of Rabbi Hillel, who allowed divorce for many reasons, and the school of Shammai, who allowed divorce for adultery alone. A sane and balanced attitude to sex questions is as difficult to find among religious teachers as elsewhere. For some religions sex is to be abhorred and the body is an enemy of the spirit. Other religions have practised temple prostitution and allowed licence. In reply to the question Jesus spoke of sex frankly, positively and with gratitude. Marriage is part of God's fundamental plan for mankind. Men and women supplement each other. Their lives are meant to merge, physically and spiritually: apart they are incomplete. When marriage is so regarded, divorce is impossible. Marriage is a lifelong indissoluble relation of love and loyalty, not a mere legal contract. Even if separated, and St. Paul understood Him to permit separation (1 Cor. 7. 10-11), husband and wife still belong together.

The longer discussion about the Jewish law of marriage and divorce is omitted by Luke, perhaps because he is writing primarily for Gentile readers. But he includes the uncompromising pronouncement about the indissolubility of marriage. 'Everyone that putteth away his wife and marrieth another, committeth adultery: and he that marrieth one that is put away from a husband committeth adultery' (16.18). Jesus was speaking to a situation where divorce was easy and in the hands of the husband alone. The question of the right of a woman to freedom from a cruel husband would not arise in the minds of his hearers. The only divorce they had heard of was of wives by husbands. The fundamental principle of Jewish law was that adultery was an offence against the property of the husband. Against this principle and against easy divorce by the husband Jesus declared that any man who divorced his wife because of lust to possess another was committing adultery. He is championing the cause of the woman. The effect of His pronouncement is to put husband and wife on a basis of equality.

Here as usual in His teaching Jesus is going behind the particular legislative issue put to Him to the fundamental principle. I see no reason to hold that here alone in His teaching He was legislating either for Church or State. Side by side in Matthew's version of the Sermon on the Mount are two passages about adultery. ' Ye have heard that it was said, Thou shalt not commit adultery; but I say unto you that everyone that looketh on a woman to lust after her hath committed adultery with her already in his heart. . . . It was said also, Whosoever shall put away his wife, let him give her a writing of divorcement, but I say unto you, that everyone that putteth away his wife, saving for the cause of fornication, maketh her an adulteress: and whosoever shall marry her when she is put away committeth adultery ' (Matt. 5.27-28, 31-32). The first passage is obviously not legislation, yet it is as uncompromising a statement as the second. Moses is not blamed for recognizing and making allowance for man's hardness of heart (Matt. 19.3-9).

Jesus was laying down the principle that sexual intimacy implies a union of personalities such that it should be life-long. In true marriage the spiritual is expressed through the physical, and the physical is subordinate to the spiritual. If not a sacrament in the strict sense, Christian marriage is yet sacramental. Those who are loyal to Him will so regard it.

The Christian ideal is clear. It is not so clear what should be done in Church or State when a marriage has failed to live up to the ideal. No Christian can regard divorce lightly as a normal and natural expedient. The situation in which divorce becomes a possibility is contrary to God's purpose for marriage. Divorce is always a tragedy, particularly for the children. Many scholars believe that the exception in Matthew is an interpretation put by the early Church upon the teaching of our Lord rather than part of the original saying. It would certainly seem contrary to the spirit of the teaching of Jesus to think of adultery as the one sin for which there was to be no forgiveness. To the Christian disciple faced by ill-treatment in marriage as elsewhere Jesus would commend the search for forgiveness and restitution. In every situation there are not only the guilty and the offended partners, but also the possibility of repentance and restitution with the help of God. Yet there are circumstances when the marriage has broken down in reality and no way of mending it is possible or desirable; and it may break down for other reasons than adultery. I do not believe that loyalty to Christ forbids us to allow divorce in such circumstances.

Certainly the Church ought only to solemnize a marriage in which the man and woman concerned accept the Christian view of marriage as a lifelong union, and enter upon it with the solemn purpose to maintain it till death shall part them.

Whatever rules the Church may think it right to make for its own members, for Christians, it must not try to impose the Christian ideal by State legislation upon those who are not Christians. Christians will strive to lead their fellow citizens to accept high ideals for marriage. It is of the greatest moment for the welfare of the community that the institution of marriage should be held in high respect, even if some hard cases cannot be avoided. Marriage is not the concern of the individual husband and wife alone. Christians will seek to secure the laws that in existing social conditions will best promote the well-being of the community. But they will not regard the ideal held up by Christ as necessarily His will for the legislation of the community.

And Christians and citizens alike will recognize the wisdom of seeking to prevent occasions for divorce from arising at all. The first duty is to uphold Christian ideals of marriage by training in the home, by preparatory instruction for marriage, and by guidance when difficulties arise. Christians will be vigilant to help in forming a healthy public opinion, through literature, drama, the film and any other available channel. Whatever their divergence on the difficult question of divorce, in this positive realm at least they should be able to unite.

VIII

JESUS THE SAVIOUR

Thou art the Way,
Hadst Thou been nothing but the goal, ·
I cannot say
If Thou hadst ever met my soul.

Alice Meynell

L UKE says that when the angel appeared to the shepherds on that first Christmas day, the burden of his 'good tidings of great joy' was the birth of a 'saviour' (2.10-11). And when Jesus was come to man's estate He summed up His mission by saying that 'the Son of Man is come to seek and to save that which was lost' (19.10). The Gospel story shows Him doing it. For a Saviour is surely one who *does* things and not only talks. Jesus acts as well as teaches. He is more than an example to be copied.

Jesus found that the trouble with men was not just ignorance or thoughtlessness. They were not utterly depraved, they knew how to do good, but often in fact they did evil, for there was a poison at work in the human heart (11.13; 6.45; cf. Mark 7.21-23). Born to be children of God they would not stay in the Father's home, they went off and denied their sonship, like the prodigal. Or if they apparently stayed at home, like the elder brother, they did not really share the Father's life or see things His way. For there are two lost sons in the parable Jesus told, not only one (15.11-32).

What did Jesus mean by 'the lost'? No doubt more than we can fully understand, but we have at least His own incomparable stories to guide us. A thing is lost when its owner is deprived of its proper use and enjoyment. A coin is lost when it cannot be used as currency or as ornament. A sheep is lost when it has strayed from the care and control of its shepherd. A son is lost when he wanders away from the fellowship of his parents. When Jesus talks by analogy of men being 'lost' to God, He means that they are lost to the divine service and fellowship; they are not in their proper place or fulfilling their true end in life of serving God and enjoying Him. And that is tragedy enough without putting meanings into the word which Jesus did not put, or going beyond the evidence of reason or revelation.

Certainly when Jesus used the word 'lost' He did not mean that the position was hopeless. The very point of the stories is that the sheep and the coin can be found, and the boy return of his own free will to the home whose door was waiting open.

The rabbis taught that God welcomed repentant sinners. Jesus said that God went out to seek them and that He was only doing as God did. 'The virtues of repentance are gloriously praised in the Rabbinic literature,' wrote the great Jewish scholar, Montefiore, 'but this direct search for and appeal to the sinner are new and moving notes of high importance and significance. The good shepherd who searches for the lost sheep and reclaims it and rejoices over it, is a new figure.'[1]

Jesus did more than preach about the good life. A teacher may teach from an arm-chair or a pulpit. Jesus, like the shepherd in His own story, went out in search, with toil and danger. He did more even than show by example the right way to live. Preaching and example by themselves are not always helpful. They may condemn without redeeming. Jesus Himself, the whole living vital personality of Him, went out in friendly sympathy to men and women; even to the 'outsiders' and the 'rotters' and the 'quislings' and to hard-hearted respectability. He was accused by His enemies of being a 'friend of publicans and sinners'. The intended slander was unjust but He bore the title as an honour. He was indeed their friend, as He was ready to be the friend of any man.

None of these outcasts thought of Him as condoning the lives they were leading. In fact it was in His presence that many of them really saw for the first time the kind of people they were. But though Jesus knew them for what they were, He did not despise them or shrink from them. They found they could talk to Him and unburden them-

[1] *The Synoptic Gospels* II, pp. 520ff.

selves. He wanted to help them and befriend them, and
hard and bitter hearts often thawed in His company. Sometimes He denounced sin. More often it was just His sheer
goodness that bore silent witness. He made sinful men and
women feel that there was still hope for them and that God
loved them.

' I am come to call sinners to repentance,' He said (5.32).
That is a frequent word in Luke's Gospel. The Greek word
meant ' thinking again ', ' changing one's mind ' about life,
and oneself, and God. It meant turning away from the
old ways and making a new beginning. He restored men to
God by making them feel the need of reconciliation and
God's readiness to take them back. He assured the penitent of forgiveness.

Some turned away from Him, preferring the darkness to
His light. Some responded to His love with hatred. But
to those who received Him He gave ' power to become the
sons of God ' (John 1.12).

1

Luke has three stories in particular which tell of Jesus
meeting with people in great need and what came of it: a
prostitute, a tax-collector, and a revolutionary.

(a) The story of the anonymous penitent prostitute
(7.36-50) is found only in Luke and is one of the most
moving in the Gospel. There is no real ground for identify-
ing this woman with Mary Magdalene, whose trouble was
probably pathological and not moral (8.2), or with Mary
of Bethany, the sister of Martha and Lazarus, about whom
another story of anointing, fundamentally different in character, is recorded by Mark (14.3-9) and John (12.1-8). It
is to be noted, by the way, that the incident took place in
the house of a Pharisee, whose invitation Jesus had
accepted. Luke tells us of two other occasions when Jesus
was entertained by Pharisees (11.37; 14.1).

Probably the transforming change had been working in
the woman before and she was now taking advantage of
an opportunity to show her gratitude. Had she perhaps
met Jesus at the party Levi gave, to introduce his old associates to Him? (5.29.)

Hearing that Jesus was having dinner in Simon's house

the woman brought a box of ointment and making her way into the semi-public room went to where He was reclining at table. She wanted, Eastern fashion, to anoint His feet as a token of respect and gratitude. But before she could get the box open her deep emotion brought a flood of tears. Forgetting all the conventions in the intensity of her feeling she let down her long hair to serve as a towel and as she bent over the feet kissed them repeatedly.

The host was sure no real prophet could allow himself to be contaminated by the touch of such a woman. But Jesus understood. In her passionate outburst Jesus saw a great love that was clear evidence that her ' many sins ' had been forgiven. ' Thy sins are forgiven,' He said gently, ' thy faith hath saved thee. Go in peace.' The woman, apparently, all the while had not said a word.

' Oh, Pharisee,' comments St. Augustine, ' thou lovest little because thou supposest that little has been forgiven thee: not because little is forgiven, but because thou thinkest that which is forgiven to be but little.'

(b) One wonders what Zacchaeus had heard about Jesus (19.1-10). At least when He came to Jericho Zacchaeus made repeated efforts to see Him: that is what the Greek says. He was a wealthy man, overseer of the local tax-collectors who were probably numerous in so important a centre; regarded somewhat enviously perhaps, even by those who hated the sight of him; ostracized by all decent people because he collected taxes for the conquerors, and with a bad reputation for extortion and sharp practice into the bargain; undersized and therefore probably unusually sensitive; not a very attractive figure on any count. Yet what was going on in his mind as he forgot his dignity and climbed up the tree to make sure of seeing Jesus?

' Zacchaeus, make haste and come down, for to-day I must abide at thy house.' So Jesus had heard about Zacchaeus too. He must have read a message in that face as He stopped and looked up into the tree: a sullen, brutalized face perhaps, but now with an eager longing on it, something more than just curiosity. And Zacchaeus scrambled down the tree full of delight, and led Jesus home.

It was an unpopular thing for Jesus to do, as He must have known. That was the worst possible place to stay if He wanted to win a good hearing for His message among the people of Jericho. Zacchaeus knew that too. This gesture of friendship appealed to his self-respect, to the buried nobility in him. It was judgment day for Zacchaeus, but the day of redemption too. We do not know all that passed between them, but we are told the outcome. For such as Zacchaeus to make so bold a decision about his money was decisive proof that he had become a new man. Salvation had come to his house.

And Jesus Himself rejoiced, for this was the kind of event that made the bells ring in heaven (15.7). This was the very object of His coming: ' to seek and so save that which is lost '.

(c) Very different again was the case of the dying bandit, but alike in illustrating Jesus' power to save men (23.39-43). The two who shared Calvary with Him were perhaps followers of Barabbas, for whom Pilate had intended that central cross. They were perhaps not so much robbers as revolutionaries, members of the underground movement against the Roman occupying power. If so, the penitent thief, as we call him, may have been a Jewish patriot, misguided perhaps but no ordinary criminal.

To the physical torment of those dragging hours was added the taunts and jeers of the crowd. Perhaps those words of abuse from those He sought to save stabbed the heart of Jesus more keenly than the nails that pierced His hands and feet. How tempting to retort with words of bitterness and denunciation. But Jesus suffered in silence. It was as if He did not hear the howling pack of human wolves.

Then suddenly among the many loud and jeering voices was one that struck a different note. ' Do you not fear even God? ' it said to the other robber. ' We are receiving the fitting punishment for our deeds. But this man has done no wrong.' Then his head turned towards the central figure. ' Jesus, remember me when thou comest in thy kingdom.' And this voice evoked an instant answer: ' Truly I tell you, you shall be with me in Paradise this very day.'

What was it that called out that astonishing act of faith from the dying robber towards one dying like himself, to all appearance in weakness and defeat? What was it that made him so sure that death was not the last word, that from the Cross Jesus would pass to a throne, that those nailed hands could bring him help? He knew nothing about doctrines of the Atonement, but he was saved by the Cross none the less. He had met with Jesus and that brief contact brought new life.

All through His ministry Jesus was thus saving men, bringing them forgiveness, bringing them to God. Perhaps the most wonderful story ever told is the one Jesus made up to help men to see that this was what God wanted Him to do above all else (15.11-32). 'Here is a tale,' He seems to say, 'of how a good father treated an erring son—or rather two erring sons. God's attitude to men is rather like that. This is the best picture I can draw in human terms of the love of God.' It might be called, The Parable of the Good Father. He is the central figure, not the prodigal son. The real pathos of the story is not in the suffering of the prodigal; it is in the sorrow of the lonely father, waiting, thinking, watching. Here is a story, hardly believable apart from the teller, about the undeserved love of God welcoming the son who returns. But even that story is not the whole Gospel. It was not then ready to be told. Its complement is the story of the seeking love of God, incarnate in Jesus, and crowned by the Cross.[1]

2

What did He do in dying more than He did by living? What made the Cross necessary? 'The Son of Man *must* suffer,' He said.

We could reply truthfully enough that the political and religious situation made death inevitable for such as He was. He might have been a leader of the people, but He refused to be the kind of Messiah they wanted. He roused the hostility of the ecclesiastics as well. He was dangerously heretical about the Law. He interfered with their prerogatives and shook people's loyalty to them. He must be silenced. And though He was not a revolutionary He played with fire when He claimed to be any kind of Messiah. That wakened the suspicion of Rome and made the political authorities allies of the ecclesiastics. So because of the

[1] In my book *The Parables of the Gospels* I have written more fully about this and the other parables of Luke.

work He had to do and the kind of world in which He had to do it, the Cross could not be avoided.

But there was an inner constraint as well. Jesus not only saw death as inevitable, He felt He was *giving* His life. He was dying with a purpose: a divine purpose. The Cross was not an unmeaning tragedy. It was the fore-ordained way for the Servant of Isaiah 53, in whom more and more He came to see a foreshadowing of Himself.[1] The Cross was not only a fate to be endured: it was a deed to be done. He went forward to the Passion not like a victim but like a challenger. The redeeming purpose of God must be given full expression.

We are not concerned here with later doctrines of the Atonement, by which men have tried to understand and interpret the meaning of the Cross. Our task is to learn what we can of the mind of Jesus Himself about His death, especially as it is revealed in the Gospel according to Luke.

We should expect that His understanding of the Cross grew, that He did not see it before Him from the very first. His life would have been unreal if He had been carrying out step by step all the time a clearly foreseen programme. The Gospels do not suggest that. It seems there were times when He hoped the nation might respond. But He learned how unstable men's enthusiasms were, how stupid they could be, how little of the seed fell on good soil, how opposition and hatred were growing.

There came a time when the Cross stood out clearly in all its starkness. Three times at least He tried to explain to His disciples how in the Messianic vocation as He had come to see it and to accept it, the death and resurrection of the Messiah were involved. These three forecasts are recorded in all the Synoptic Gospels. It is possible that some of the details were added to the story in the light of the event; insensibly perhaps the story would be coloured by the way it actually happened. But that does not affect the central fact that during the later days of His ministry Jesus declared that the triumph of the Kingdom of God depended upon His death.

(*a*) The turning point in the ministry seems to have been

[1] Cf. 22.37 and Isa. 53.12: a further clear indication of His mind on the eve of the Cross.

Peter's confession, the rock on which the Church is built (9.18-27). Jesus asked the disciples the challenging question: Who am I? Spokesman of the little band, Peter gives the answer: You are God's Messiah. They had lived with Him in the fullest intimacy and had watched Him at work and in His hours of leisure. Gradually the conviction of His unique Lordship had forced itself on them. In hailing Him as Messiah they were giving Him the highest place they could conceive, as the one in whom all the promises of God came to fruition.

Matthew's Gospel (16.13-20) brings out more clearly than Luke's the importance of this moment and the joy with which Jesus hailed this recognition. The time was still not ripe for any public announcement which would only lend itself to popular misunderstanding. Yet a momentous hour had struck. Unlike though He was to the popular conceptions of the Messiah, His own followers understood, so far at least, who He was and what was His task.

But now they had a further and even harder lesson to learn. They had acknowledged Him as the Messiah. He accepted the title. But now for the first time He shared with them the conviction that had been growing in His own mind; the Messiah will be rejected and put to death, to rise again. He is going to Jerusalem. If they are going to follow they must take their lives in their hands, like a criminal carrying the bar of his own cross to execution. It is a summons to loyalty and adventure—to dangerous living; not an exhortation to asceticism.

Looking back with all the associations that have gathered around the Cross it is impossible for us to appreciate how startled and shocked the disciples must have been. 'The Messiah must suffer.' It did not make sense. No Jew had ever thought in such terms. The only Old Testament passage which might be so understood was Isaiah 53, and no Jew then or since has taken that as referring to the Messiah. Again Matthew and Mark help us to understand the horror of the disciples (Matt. 16.22-23; Mark 8.32-33) at this overthrow of all their hopes. It is a marvel that only one mutinied. (See also Deut. 21.22-23.)

(b) Later in the same chapter (9.28-45) Luke tells us how Jesus warned the disciples again. Some of them had shared with Him the intense exultation of the Transfiguration.

There is mystery here which we cannot rationalize if we would. At least it meant a re-dedication to His task and a reassurance of the divine approval of His choice of the way of the Cross. For the three disciples, too, it seems that ' the veil of sense ' that shrouds spiritual reality was drawn aside while Jesus prayed. There had followed a striking cure of an epileptic boy. Jesus told them not to be misled by the popular applause. The end of the ministry would be re-jection. And still they wouldn't believe it.

(c) The third warning (18.31-34) is given a vivid introduc-tion in Mark's account (10.32). It is a scene for a great painter to interpret. They were on their way to Jerusalem. But Jesus was striding ahead of them, His face set (9.53; Isa. 50.7), with a lonely determination of soul they could not share. And they were frightened as they followed Him; this was something new and strange in their experience. Once more Jesus tried to explain to them what lay ahead: ill-treatment and death, but after that a resurrection. He is marching on Jerusalem for that last terrible conflict where Love unarmed save with its own weapons is to meet evil in a death grapple; pride, greed, cruelty, prejudice, fear, in horrible array. Jerusalem, He had said with sad irony, is the only proper place for a prophet to die (13.31-35). As they looked back the disciples were astonished at their own blindness and lack of understanding.

3

Three great symbolic actions, akin in spirit to the dramatic symbolism of the Old Testament prophets, pre-face the story of the Passion, each bearing witness to Christ's thought about His death.

(a) His entry to Jerusalem was a clear public claim to be Messiah (19.28-40), but an equally clear assertion that His way was peace not armed rebellion. No doubt most of those who acclaimed Him were His own folk from Galilee, but there might well be others from among the great throngs of pilgrims who were there at the time. There is no need to imagine that it was these same voices that cried ' crucify Him! ' from the packed jury before Pilate. This entry was an acted parable. Out of all the Messianic prophecies in the Scriptures He chose one that told of the

King coming to Jerusalem riding upon an ass, not upon a
war horse. (See Zechariah 9.9-10.) He was to destroy the
weapons of war and yet win ' dominion from sea to sea, and
from the river even to the ends of the earth '.

(b) When He reached Jerusalem He strode through the
Court of the Gentiles in the Temple scattering the desecrat-
ing traders before the hurricane of His indignation, like a
prophetic symbol of God coming to His Temple to sweep
out false religion. It was one man against a host but they
were cowed by His moral authority (19.45-46). But it rallied
His enemies against Him.

(c) Third and greatest symbol of the significance of His
Passion was the Last Supper with His disciples (22.7-20).[1]
The Cross was a deliberately chosen means of sealing the
new covenant between God and man of which Jeremiah
had spoken (Jer. 31.31-34) and to the establishment of
which all His life had been devoted.[2] He made the bread
and the wine of the Supper symbols of His life willingly
laid down. The Lord's Supper is so rich in meaning and
symbolism that no one metaphor can exhaust it. But this
is one meaning that Jesus Himself put into it. It is the
new covenant in His blood: evidence of God's desire to
enter into new and closer fellowship with us. When we
take the cup we enter into this covenant with God, to be
His loyal servants, to obey His laws, to reverence His name
and to live in justice and mercy with our fellows.

There is no need here to attempt to retell Luke's story of
the Passion itself. Better to lay down this book and read
again the incomparable words that record those supreme
hours with such power and telling restraint.

The New Testament doctrine of salvation is not only
illustrated by the historic facts of the Cross and Passion.

---

[1] For present purposes we can disregard the much debated
questions (a) whether this was the Passover meal itself, as Luke
apparently thought, or one on the day before the Passover, as the
Fourth Gospel says; (b) whether, as seems likely, the original text
of Luke has had phrases added to it from the other New Testament accounts.

[2] For a vivid picture of the ratification of the old covenant see
Exodus 24.3-8. The thought of the covenant runs right through the
Old Testament, which indeed is named after it, as the New Testa-
ment (or covenant) is named after the new.

It arose out of those facts. At first the Cross was a stumbling block, the wreck of the disciples' hopes. But they came to see it as Jesus had seen it, as the essential plan of God in a sinful world. A Messiah on a cross! Yes, ' God commendeth His love toward us, in that while we were yet sinners, Messiah died for us.' (Rom. 5.8).

IX

THE RISEN JESUS

Christ when He died
Deceived the crosse,
And on death's side
Threw all the losse:
The captive world awak't and found
The prisoners loose, the jailor bound.

O strange mysterious strife,
Of open death and hidden life:
When on the crosse my king did bleed,
Life seemed to die, Death died indeed.

Richard Crashaw

BETWEEN the feasts of Passover and Pentecost something stupendous must have happened. In his second volume Luke describes how Peter delivered a public speech in Jerusalem, supported by the other apostles, and boldly making the most astonishing claims on behalf of Jesus. Yet it was only the other day that Jesus had been executed in this very city, with Peter disowning any knowledge of Him. Something must have happened.

The ministry of Jesus of Nazareth ended in failure. He died the death of a criminal at the hands of Roman law after having been denounced by His own countrymen. Jeered at by His enemies, betrayed by one of His intimate chosen band, denied by another, forsaken by nearly all, He spent His last hours in torture. As night fell on Calvary the black shadow of despair lay on all who had loved Him. They were broken-hearted at the unutterable outrage done to their friend and master. And there must have been bitter searchings of heart about their own behaviour.

He had tried to prepare them for this: He had told them more than once that He was going to His death. But they had never really taken it in. They believed that He was God's promised Messiah and yet He had ended on a cross between two thieves. It just didn't make sense. They must face the facts: Jesus was dead and buried. Not merely sorrow filled their hearts but the assurance of utter defeat. When the sun rose on Easter morning they were convinced that the whole business was ended. The women of the little group were going to perform the last customary offices of love, to embalm with myrrh and spices the dead body of the leader of a lost cause.

Then something happened; something stupendous enough to change defeat into triumph, and transform broken men into heroes. The men who had run for their lives forsaking their master, now stand before a great crowd, confident and unflinching. Their spokesman is the Peter who could not face the banter of a servant girl. Among the apostles at his side is doubting Thomas, who had declared that with the Cross all hope had vanished, and had refused to be comforted even when his fellows had been convinced.

The little band was already one hundred and twenty strong. It was soon to add three thousand to its number. Henceforth no threats of ecclesiastical authority, no popular prejudice, no experience of prison or the lash or the threat of death could break their brave front. The very Cross that had meant disgrace and disaster now inspired them with courage.

Something must have happened adequate to effect so astonishing a transformation.

1

It is true that the story as told in the Gospels is not easy to follow. They present at least two lines of apparently independent tradition not readily reconcilable. If this was a made-up story these are stupid lapses. But they may rather be the result of honest testimony to an unexpected and unparalleled event which dumbfounded the witnesses. Sworn depositions immediately after the event from reliable eye-witnesses would have produced just such discrepancies.

In addition to variations in the story of the first appearances there are clearly two collections of stories, centred respectively in Jerusalem and in Galilee. Luke's own account, though he must have been familiar with the tradition embodied in the lost ending of Mark's Gospel, is notably independent of the others. Of his fifty-three verses only sixteen have any parallel in the other Gospels. The different sets of stories are not clearly related to one another and with our present knowledge we cannot neatly dovetail them together. There are even discrepancies between Luke's own two accounts in the Gospel and in the Acts. But there is no adequate reason for regarding the stories as contradictory: they are rather independent and supplementary. The very divergences are evidence that the Church was not relying upon a concocted tale. It is notorious that false witnesses usually take pains to agree on the same story. What is beyond question is that while the discrepancies relate to details, there is unanimity of testimony as to the main fact: ' He showed himself alive after his passion by many infallible proofs ' (Acts 1.3). Each evangelist tells representative stories, no doubt in each case a selection from a larger available number, to bring home the central significance of the great fact of the Resurrection. The details of time and place were of quite secondary importance in the mind of the evangelists, and may well be so in ours.

Here again, as so often, one cannot fail to be impressed by the restraint and reticence of the Gospel narrative. No attempt is made, for example, to describe the actual Resurrection itself. Some of the apocryphal gospels show what an unrestrained fancy might make of it. Imagine even a literary genius set to describe what a risen Jesus might have done and said. Would any romancer have produced such a tale as Luke tells?

It is well to remember that the earliest written testimony we possess to the Resurrection comes from the Apostle Paul, whose epistles preceded all the Gospels. (Though of course documents underlying the Gospels may have been earlier still.) Paul staked the Christian Faith on the truth of the Resurrection. In almost all his letters there are statements taking it for granted, without argument, that Christ had died but was alive again. Fortunately, however, for later ages there was a debate in the Corinthian Church, not so much about the Resurrection of Christ as about the doctrine of immortality. So Paul is led in writing to them to discuss the Resurrection and to give a summary of the facts (1 Cor. 15.1-8).

The First Letter to the Corinthians was perhaps written in A.D. 55 but this testimony carries us back long before that. The apostle says this was what he told them on his visit five or six years before. It was the common Christian belief which he had received when he himself became a Christian; that is, four or five years after the death of Jesus. He had been transformed from a bitter opponent and persecutor of the Christian Faith into its leading advocate. And Paul was certainly one of the most acute minds of that or of any generation, accustomed by training and temperament to make short work of insubstantial arguments. He was a contemporary of these events and in a position to investigate the facts. He would not have been easy to convince.

2

The two fundamental and well-attested facts are (a) that the tomb of Jesus was found empty, and (b) that He Himself appeared alive after His death to various individuals and groups of His disciples. On these two facts all four evangelists and St. Paul are agreed. Here we are primarily concerned with the story as Luke tells it in the light of his investigations (23.50-24).

(a) Jesus was buried hastily by Joseph of Arimathea in a tomb owned by him near the place of crucifixion. It was necessary to complete the burial by sunset when the Sabbath began, and it was therefore impossible to prepare the body in accordance with Jewish custom. So the women who had followed His body to the tomb returned at dawn, after the Sabbath, bringing with them the spices for the embalming. To their grief and astonishment they found the body gone. Two men ' in dazzling apparel ', probably angels, announced that Jesus was alive and had risen from the dead.

The women reported all this to the eleven, who refused to believe the story. They said the women were overwrought and delirious and had imagined it. But Peter ran to the tomb, accompanied according to the Fourth Gospel by John, and saw for himself that it was empty, except for the linen grave clothes. The presence of the clothes was surprising. If the body had been taken away, whether by friends or enemies, why had the wrappings been left behind? The account in the Fourth Gospel implies that the clothes were lying not in a heap but just as if the body had disappeared from them, like a sheath from which the sword had been withdrawn. The head bandage was lying by itself on the ledge where the head had lain.

Peter went home wondering what had happened. There is no suggestion that the discovery of the empty tomb in itself created belief in the Resurrection, except in the case of John (John 20.8). The others were puzzled, startled, distressed. The empty tomb is stated as a fact, not advanced as a proof or an argument.

All four evangelists agree that the tomb was empty, except for the clothes, when the women went at dawn, that the women were completely surprised and that the disciples refused to believe their story. All agree that someone in white told the women that Jesus was risen. The discrepancies are of minor importance.

There are no textual reasons for doubting this story: it is part of the originals. There is no reason for disbelieving Luke or the others when they tell us the tomb was empty, if we accept them, as we have every reason to do, as honest reporters.

Why was the tomb empty? It is incredible that the disciples stole the body. If for some inexplicable reason a group of them had removed it, could the secret possibly have been kept? There is no reason why the Romans should have removed it. It is childish to suggest that the women went by mistake to the wrong tomb. If His enemies stole the body they would certainly have produced it to stifle the new faith at its birth; they used every means available, including murder. If the body was not produced it could only be because it was not available.

(b) The second well-attested fact is that Jesus appeared alive after His death on several occasions. What the apostles proclaimed was not that Jesus was alive in heaven but that He was risen and that they had seen Him and heard Him.

According to Luke (24.13-35) the first actually to see the risen Jesus were two disciples, not members of the eleven, who were making their sad way home to Emmaus. This story of imperishable beauty we owe to Luke's inquiries.

It bears all the marks of being recorded for him by one of the participants. The two, perhaps husband and wife, were talking over together the tragic disillusionment of the past days. A stranger overtook them and inquired the subject of their conversation. They were surprised at the suggestion that there could be more than one possible topic. For them and surely for all Jerusalem one event overshadowed all else, the crucifixion of Jesus of Nazareth, the great prophet: they could no longer call Him Messiah, though once they had cherished that hope. It was true that some of the women had told extraordinary stories about angels, which apparently they did not believe, though the fact of the tomb being empty had been confirmed.

The stranger told them that such sufferings were only to be expected for the Messiah, as the Scriptures made clear. When they reached their home they urged Him to come and take supper with them. He agreed. Something characteristic in the way He blessed and broke the bread revealed to them who He was. Then ' He vanished out of their sight '.

Once again, may it not be urged, this story is not the stuff of imagination. Here is a simple unadorned narrative with the surprising, even rather unconvincing, statement that they did not recognize Him. That has the unexpectedness of reality but it is not the way an inventor would have told it.

So momentous an experience must be shared, and without delay. They returned at once to Jerusalem to tell the apostles. Even before they could report what had happened they found the little company already transformed. Jesus had appeared to Simon and the change in him was evidence enough to convince the others. And then the two had their own story to add.

Then Jesus Himself appeared in the midst of them (24.36-43) suddenly, ' out of nowhere,' as we say, with the customary Jewish greeting of ' Peace '. A succession of violent emotions seized the company; fright at the sudden apparition passing into a feeling that this could not be true, that it was too good to be true. Patiently Jesus set Himself to persuade, showing them His hands and His feet with the wounds of the nails still visible. It was recognizably Himself, yet now the matter of His body was so at the command of His spirit that He could enter a closed room, appear and vanish at will. Luke even says that He asked for food and ate in their presence. To us this seems incongruous and hard to understand. If this be an accurate memory, we must suppose that Jesus ate the food not because He needed it but in order to calm and convince the company. Perhaps it was necessary that sign should be added to sign; after the empty tomb, the display of the hands and feet, the invitation to feel the solid flesh, the eating and drinking. The nature of the resurrection body of Jesus is beyond our comprehension. We must frankly admit that here we are in a realm of mystery upon mystery, confronting a unique event where our normal experience cannot guide us nor the methods of science help.

But if the whole narrative of the Resurrection presents us with unparalleled events, what then? For Jesus Himself is unparalleled in human experience. Science could only deny the Resurrection if it could claim to have compassed and understood all reality.

To the reassured and convinced company Jesus explained, as to the two on the road to Emmaus, the divine necessity and fitness of all that had happened. They were to be witnesses of all these things to all nations, and for this task beyond human resources they would receive an endowment of power (24.44-49).

At first sight it would seem as if Luke means us to understand that the walk to Bethany and the Ascension followed immediately on the evening of Easter Day. But we know from Luke himself in the Acts, and from the other Gospels, that it was not so. It is clear that the whole narrative is greatly condensed, and Luke may not even mean to convey that all the instructions and explanations were given by Jesus at that first meeting.

Luke is our only authority for the account of the Ascension which, according to Acts, did not take place for some 'forty days' after Easter. His brief account in the Gospel (24.50-53) is expanded in Acts (1.6-11). Jesus evidently made it clear to the company that this 'vanishing' was to be the end of His appearances to their physical senses. We are not, of course, to picture a physical ascent to a heaven placed above the clouds. It was a symbolical withdrawal after a solemn benediction.

3

The whole story of the Resurrection is in the nature of things unprecedented and inevitably beyond our comprehension. Details may be open to legitimate question but we have to choose between accepting the story as substantially true, or believing in a most extraordinary series of blunders. Any suggestion of deliberate fraud on the part of the disciples can be dismissed. There is no reason to challenge the sincerity of the story. If it is not true, then men and women, who expected nothing of the kind, believed the tomb to be empty when in fact it was not. If it is not true, several individuals and groups at varied times and in varied circumstances believed that they saw Jesus alive, when in fact they did not. And this series of blunders so transformed these people that they started the Christian Church on an amazing enterprise against impossible odds, which has carried it in this twentieth century literally to the very ends of the earth. This is not how hallucinations work.

The New Testament stories of the Resurrection are fundamentally convincing and they will stand the closest scrutiny. But the greatest and most convincing testimony to the reality of the Resurrection is the birth and vitality of the Christian Church emerging out of the amazing transformation that came to a little group of beaten and despairing men.

If Luke had not been able to write the last chapter of his Gospel, he would not have been able to write the book of the Acts of the Apostles at all. For if there had been no Resurrection there would have been no apostles. Belief in the Resurrection created the Church before any of our Gospels were written, and apart from belief in the Resurrection they would never have been written at all. The surge of new life that came into the world in the first century of our era, and that pulses through every page of the New Testament, is quite inexplicable if the Resurrection is not a fact.

X

JESUS THE LORD

The very God! think, Abib; dost thou think?
So, the All-great were the All Loving too—
So, through the thunder comes a human voice
Saying, 'O heart I made, a heart beats here,
Face my hands fashioned, see it in myself!
Thou hast no power nor may'st conceive of mine,
But love I gave thee, with myself to love,
And thou must love me who have died for thee?'
       An Epistle of Karshish, Robert Browning

NOTHING in the Gospel story is more startling—or to many people more unwelcome—than the self-assertion of Jesus. The great religious teachers of mankind have usually pointed to the truths they taught and not to themselves. The greater the saint the more self-effacing he is. But we must reckon with the fact that Jesus put Himself in the forefront of His message; more, declared that He Himself was the message.

Emerson is alleged to have complained that 'the history of Christianity has dwelt with noxious exaggeration on the person of Christ'. One sometimes meets people who say they wish Christians would drop their complicated creeds and theological dogmas and stick to 'the simple teaching of the Sermon on the Mount'. It may be questioned whether that teaching is in fact very simple, either to understand or to obey. In any case it does not allow us to escape the person of the teacher. For here, in the Sermon on the Mount, is one who declares that He supersedes and corrects the divinely inspired law of Moses. 'It hath been said . . . but I say.' And at the last He declares that the only hope for men is to base their lives on the rock foundation of 'my sayings' (6.47-49).

Ranged round the walls at the headquarters of the Theosophical Society at Adyar, near Madras, are statues of the world's great religious leaders; Krishna, the Buddha,

Zoroaster, and a motley group—and Jesus. That is the characteristic spirit of Hinduism, and there are some superficial people who think such a proceeding ' broad-minded '. But Jesus does not allow Himself to be set in a row with others.

It would be good if we could rid ourselves for a time of our familiarity with the words of the Gospels and the claims of the Christian Faith and simply submit ourselves to the impact of the Gospel facts and see where they would take us. Any sincere study of the Gospel of Luke, or of any Gospel, will bring us face to face with the ultimate enigma of the personality of Jesus and His self-knowledge.

1

Let us look more closely at the claims that Jesus made, according to this Gospel.

(1) He claimed to be the Messiah, that is, the fulfilment of the promises of God through the prophets, the pivot on which history turned. He was different from all God's earlier messengers and prophets, as the heir is different from the servants (20.9-19). With the coming of Jesus, a new era dawns, the Kingdom of God is here. ' Blessed are the eyes which see the things that ye see: for I say unto you that many prophets and kings desired to see the things which ye see and saw them not; and to hear the things which ye hear, and heard them not ' (10.23-24). ' Your eyes,' He said; not ' our eyes '. The blessing is one He brings, not one He shares with them. As we have seen His entry to Jerusalem was a deliberate claim to Messiahship (19.29-38).

' This day ' with my appearing—' is this scripture fulfilled ' (4.21). The Kingdom of God has come to earth: it is no more an aspiration and a dream.

(2) He claimed that His teaching superseded the teaching of the elders and of the Law, in whose divine origin both He and His hearers believed. Till John the law and the prophets: now He supersedes both (16.16). The scribes say, ' It is written '. The prophets declare, ' Thus saith the Lord '. Here is one who says, ' But I say ' (6.27). He said ' Come to me ' when any other would have said ' Return unto the Lord our God '.

(3) He claimed to forgive sins. ' Man, thy sins are for-

given thee' (5.20). Sinlessness is a negative word to apply
to such a personality as His. Say rather that He showed
Himself adequate to every situation and demand, with a
consecration without reserve to His Father's will. It is
positive words like heroism, devotion, goodness, love that
we want to use of Him. Yet here is the strange and unprecedented fact. Usually the greater the saint, the keener
his repentance and the more pronounced his consciousness
of falling short of his high ideals. Jesus exposed and rebuked
sin with a sternness only equalled by His gentleness with the
penitent, and He called men urgently to repentance. But we
have no confessions from the lips of Jesus Himself. Never,
to encourage His disciples, did He tell the story of any
experience of repentance and change of heart in Himself,
or of what God's forgiveness had done for Him. He exer-
cised and defended His right to forgive the sins of others
with a tone of final authority. He never sought forgiveness
for Himself.

(4) Profounder than even such claims as these and point-
ing to mysteries even less to be plumbed, is the claim
implied by what Jesus tells us of His own knowledge of
Himself.

Jesus lived and moved and had His being in a habitual
consciousness of the presence of God and was consumed by
a passion for the realization of the divine purpose of redemption for mankind. To put this in other words: He had
a sense of perfect harmony with the holiness and love of
God and a complete consecration and dedication to His
Kingdom. And He knew that in this He was far different
from other men around Him. God was His Father in a
sense which was true of no one else. He distinguished between His sonship and that of others. He spoke of 'my
Father' and 'your Father' but never of 'our Father' when
He was including others with Himself (cf. 12.30,32; 10.22).

Indeed the distinctive teaching of Christianity is not that
God is the Father of everybody but that He is the Father
of Jesus. It was because of His unique consciousness of
sonship that He called men to learn the secret of sonship
from Himself. The clearest expression of this is to be found
in 10.21ff.: 'All things have been delivered unto me of my
Father: and no one knoweth who the Son is, save the
Father; and who the Father is, save the Son, and he to

whomsoever the Son willeth to reveal him.' He claimed to stand in a unique relationship both to God and to man. He knew God as no other did and had the power to convey that knowledge.

We have already seen how at the baptism the call to Messiahship was linked with His consciousness of a peculiar relationship to God. It was out of that that His vocation arose. Luke (3.21-22) brings out clearly the personal and spiritual experience behind the vocation.

The parable of the vineyard (20.9-19) implies unmistakably the same sense of difference. In His thought about Himself Jesus was not merely a prophet, not simply a man who had progressed further than others in the understanding of God. 'Men there have been,' wrote Sir George Adam Smith, 'who felt themselves able to say "I know" and who died like Him for their convictions. But He was able to say "I am: I am that to which prophecy has pointed" and was able to feel Himself worthy to be that.'[1] In Him something new had happened in history.

This self-knowledge of Jesus so expressed is one element in the evidence that compelled the Church later to formulate the doctrine of the Trinity and of the divinity of Christ. The Church was right in so doing. Yet while one dare not dogmatize it must seem very unlikely that Jesus Himself in the days of His flesh fully knew the secret of His own being. The relationship was intuitive, moral and spiritual: not even, one may dare to think, in the mind of Jesus were its theological and metaphysical implications fully realized.

The incarnation was a reality. God chose to reveal Himself as a Galilean peasant of a particular generation. Jesus lived a real human life with the inevitable human limitations. He grew mentally as well as physically. He learned by experience, through joy and love, through suffering and through temptation. His prayers were real. The agony in the garden was real. For a moment on the Cross He even believed Himself deserted by God. All the while He knew that He was more and other than His fellow men. He was conscious of an intimate fellowship with God which He found other men did not share. But if Jesus Himself had been conscious of His Godhead could the incarnation have been other than the playing of a part? 'He emptied

[1] *Jerusalem* 2, p. 584.

Himself, taking the form of a servant, being made in the likeness of men ' (Phil. 2.7).

Jesus nowhere said ' I am God '. He did not propound any doctrine of divinity about Himself, but He did naturally and without apology what only God can properly do. He acted as plenipotentiary for God. And He made the most unmistakable and unqualified claims to occupy a unique status in relation both to God and to man. Though they are never formulated by Jesus Himself, His own thoughts about Himself involved in the end the doctrines of the incarnation and the atonement and the Trinity.

(5) It is hardly strange that one who could so speak of Himself and His vocation should claim from men an utter allegiance. Yet only familiarity could allow us to listen to His summons without awe and amazement. He called men to face disinheritance, persecution, hatred, death, ' for my name's sake ': and yet, sublime paradox, He assured them that though they died not a hair of their head would perish, nothing could harm *them*, their real selves (21.12-19).

After He had warned His disciples that the path of the Messiah led inevitably to rejection and death, He called them to follow Him upon the path with, as we might say, the halter already round their necks. ' If any man would come after me, let him deny himself and take up his cross daily and follow me. For whosoever would save his life shall lose it, but whosoever shall lose his life for my sake, the same shall save it. For what is a man profited, if he gain the whole world and lose or forfeit his own self? For whosoever shall be ashamed of me and of my words, of him shall the Son of Man be ashamed when he cometh in his own glory, and the glory of the Father and of the holy angels ' (9.23-26). When ' great multitudes ' crowded after Him with superficial enthusiasm, He warned them of the cost of discipleship: ' If any man cometh unto me and hateth not his own father, and mother, and wife and children, and brethren, and sisters, yea, and his own life also, he cannot be my disciple. Whosoever doth not bear his own cross and come after me, cannot be my disciple ' (14. 25-27).

Who can He be who uses words like these? Custom has dulled their force for us. But if we take time to realize what they mean, we shall want to know by what authority a man could make such claims? If they are not justified they are madness or blasphemy? 'He is either God or He is not a good man' is an ancient dilemma. Is it not true?

2

Yet the men who knew Jesus best allowed these claims. The New Testament was written because they accepted them. The inner group of disciples kept close company with Jesus for two or three years. They were in daily contact, living together in public and private, on duty and off, in happiness and in trouble. They were near enough to note every flaw. Yet the time came when Peter realized that his familiar friend was different. 'Depart from me, for I am a sinful man, O Lord' (5.8). 'Thou art the Christ of God' (9.18-20).

One can trace throughout the Gospel the cumulative impression made upon them by the personality of Jesus. For example, after the cure of the paralytic (5.17-26) 'amazement took hold on all, and they glorified God; and they were filled with fear, saying, We have seen strange things to-day'. After the storm on the Lake, 'being afraid, they marvelled, saying one to another, Who then is this, that he commandeth even the winds and the water and they obey him?' (8.25; cf. 9.34, 43-45). Such experiences led to the need to attempt later theological formulation. They were awed and baffled, but there is yet no dogma or theory. In the Gospels we can see the disciples beginning to try to express what they believed about Jesus.

Momentous in this process is Peter's confession at Caesarea Philippi. Luke tells us of the incident, but it is to Mark that we owe our knowledge of the place where it took place. For us looking back there seems something peculiarly fitting and dramatic in the setting. It is near the source of the Jordan and was already in the time of Jesus a great centre of religious and political interest. Here was a grotto sacred to the nymphs and to Pan, the god of nature and the natural instincts. Before the Greeks came there it was dedicated to the worship of the Baalim, the old gods of the land. Nearby was a white temple, consecrated to the worship of the Roman emperor, erected by Herod after the

visit of Caesar Augustus; a temple in fact for the worship
of the State.[1] One cannot help seeing in Peter's confession,
the rock on which the Christian Church arose, a challenge
to these two ancient religions, of nature and the absolute
State; religions not yet dead.

For here, after prayer, Jesus put a searching question to
the little group. They had been with Him long enough now
and intimately enough to have made their judgment. They
had lived beside Him, heard His teaching, seen Him in
action, shared His intimate thoughts. They knew the vary-
ing verdicts passed upon Him by other people. ' Who do *you*
say I am? ' asked Jesus. And Peter as spokesman for them
all dared to acclaim Him as ' Christ of God ', the Messiah,
utterly unlike though He was to men's preconceived notions
of Messiahship. To say this, was to set Jesus above the
prophets, as the supreme envoy and representative of God,
the culmination of history and the key to the future. Jesus
was deeply moved. The confession showed that His teaching had not been altogether in vain. They had grasped
something at least of His great secret. Here at last was the
nucleus of the company who would carry on His purposes
when the Cross had claimed Him. Matthew's Gospel
(16.13-23) brings out the significance of the occasion more
clearly than Luke does, but in all three Synoptic Gospels
this confession is the great turning point in the ministry.

Jesus was not understood by the disciples all at once.
There was a growing sense of His graciousness, mysterious-
ness, authority. When they came at last to recognize Him
as Messiah, they gave Him the highest human title they
had to give, but it was still human. It was a struggle for
Jews to adjust their belief in Jesus to their belief in God.
In Peter's speeches in Acts 2-4 Jesus is still apparently
just the Messiah. But Stephen's dying words imply a further
step: 'Lord Jesus, receive my spirit' (Acts 7.59). He was
quoting, as Jesus had quoted at the end, from Psalm 31.
But he put the name of Jesus in place of the name of God.
' Here the first Christian to die commended his spirit to
Jesus. It is a devotional not a dogmatic utterance; but its
implications will need a whole theology to state them. It
is a devotional equation of Jesus with the God of the spirits

[1] See G. A. Smith, *Historical Geography of the Holy Land*,
p. 474.

of all flesh. It is characteristic of the growth of Christian theology that religious experience should precede dogmatic formula.'[1]

As soon as men saw God in Christ problems arose which led to the formulation of the doctrine of the Trinity in the attempt to explain them. Christians found themselves driven by their experience to belief in the divinity of Christ. ' We have not here a perplexing dogma imposed by authority upon men's reluctant minds; what we have is a triumphant discovery based on experience as all scientific truth must be based. They use religious and devotional language which completely implies the doctrine of the Godhead of Jesus Christ before they state that doctrine in set terms. The experience comes first; the formulation comes later.'[2]

These men had nothing to gain by admitting the claims of Jesus, and everything to lose. It led them to ridicule, hardship, loss and martyrdom. There must have been overwhelming evidence to produce this conviction in such men. And it must be remembered that they were Jews with a horror of even mentioning another name beside that of the eternal God. ' The grace of the Lord Jesus Christ, the love of God, and the fellowship of the Holy Spirit '; what an amazing sentence to be written by a Jew, and by one who had started as a bitter enemy of the Christian cause with all his prejudices, traditions and interests against the acknowledgement of the claims of Jesus.

' Jesus is Lord! ' That was where the facts inexorably led the first disciples. Where ought they to lead us?

[1] Temple, *Christus Veritas*, p. 108.
[2] *Op. cit.*, p. 112.

H

XI

FOLLOWING JESUS

May we, having seen God's Beauty,
live henceforth in Love,
by the merit of Faith toiling to endow the world,
offering all our service at the throne of God.
The Testament of Beauty (iii. 241ff.), Robert Bridges

THERE are many other questions about the person and teaching of Jesus which we might ask of St. Luke's Gospel, but which space forbids discussing here. And there are some very important questions about which Luke says little or nothing, for which we must look elsewhere in the New Testament. But there is one concluding question which must not be omitted: What does it mean to follow Jesus? What did Jesus ask of His disciples and what did He promise them? Much of the answer will consist in a kind of survey and summary from a new angle of subjects we have already considered in previous chapters.

1

We have already seen the demand Jesus made for absolute loyalty. The cost of discipleship varies from generation to generation and from man to man, but always He asks for utter loyalty. When Luke inserts the word ' daily ' in Jesus' saying (9.23) we see perhaps the desire to make it apply to later generations and to use cross-bearing metaphorically. But it was no metaphor when Jesus first used it. He was asking His friends to face death along with Him, to carry the beam of the Cross at His side as condemned criminals did on the way to crucifixion; as He Himself was to do so soon on the way to Calvary. From most of us Jesus does not ask so much. But discipleship has meant precisely that for many Christians in many lands during the last few years. The age of martyrdom is not over. Jesus asks of us the readiness for even that, should the need arise.

Nor does He ask most of us to leave our homes and our work for His sake. It was only a few chosen men whom He summoned to give up everything to follow (5.1-11; 5.27-28; 9.57-62). He did not require everyone to surrender his possessions as He did the rich young ruler (18.18-27). Most of His disciples are called to follow Him in the life of the family, the field, and the workshop. There is no suggestion in His teaching that Christians generally should withdraw from society. But He did ask for readiness to go all the way with Him in an allegiance that was stronger than all the ties of even the family, whose claims He rated so highly. This challenge is stated in characteristic dramatic metaphor (14.25-35). He does not call for renunciation because He denies the value of life, nor for suffering for its own sake, but only when needed in uncompromising protest against evil and unflinching loyalty to righteousness.

Jesus loved the enthusiast, the man who knew what side he was on and threw himself wholeheartedly into the business. He liked energetic action, as in the men who climbed the roof and broke a way through for their paralysed friend (5.18-26) or in Zacchaeus who forgot his dignity and swarmed up a tree (19.1-10). He loved the generous giver. All four Gospels quote His saying, ' He who loves life loses it: he who spends keeps.' It sums up His attitude to life (9.24; cf. Matt. 16.25; Mark 8.35; John 12.25). He praised the man who banged on the door till he got an answer (11.5-8); He wanted men to show that kind of determination in the affairs of religion (11.9-13). He praised the widow who badgered the unjust judge into doing justice (18.1-8). He did not like playing for safety (19.20-26). It is the peace-makers rather than the peace-keepers whom He blesses. Goodness is a positive active loyalty.

2

Christian discipleship is not a matter of observing a set of rules, least of all a set of prohibitions. If Jesus had drawn up a set of rules for His first followers they would rapidly have become irrelevant for later generations. But there is a much deeper reason than that: the inherent nature of the Christian faith is incompatible with a religion of rules. This is explicitly brought out in Matthew's account of the

Sermon on the Mount where Jesus illustrates the inadequacy of the Mosaic Law and the traditions built on it. All right so far as they went, they did not express true righteousness: they needed to be fulfilled (Matt. 5.17-18). Luke writing for a Gentile audience does not discuss the Jewish Law but he presents the same picture of the positive teaching of Jesus. What Jesus brought was not so much a new law as the abrogation of all law. A man may know all the rules of good conduct and not keep them. He may keep all the rules and yet be proud and unloving in his relations with others. Jesus came to change the man himself, not the rules.

He gives us no systematic ethical teaching. Most of His sayings are spoken to meet the particular situation of a particular man. There is none of the casuistry and desic-cated analysis of motives of the textbooks. His sayings are illustrations which must be interpreted in the light of His governing belief in God. Our more prosaic Western minds are in danger of seriously misunderstanding Him by taking literally His picturesque Oriental language; especially if we lack a sense of humour. When He speaks of faith like a grain of mustard seed, tells us that He saw Satan fall from heaven, or that He came to bring not peace but a sword, He is using poetic metaphors not expounding theology. Perhaps even the evangelists, though orientals, at times interpreted His poetry all too prosaically. When He tells us to turn the other cheek or to go a second mile He is not legislating. Indeed it is not difficult to imagine circum-stances in which literal obedience to His sayings would be wrong. He tells us that we are not worthy of the Kingdom if we do not hate our fathers and mothers; but He also tells us that it is wrong to attempt to excuse our neglect of our fathers and mothers by saying that we had been serving God instead! (Cf. 14.26; Mark 7.8-13.) Literalism might quote Jesus as forbidding public worship (Matt. 6.6).

Jesus said that everyone who was angry with his brother was in danger of the judgment and whoever said 'thou fool' was in danger of the hell of fire (Matt. 5.22). But it is re-corded that He Himself once looked at a synagogue con-gregation 'with anger, being grieved at the hardening of their hearts' (Mark 3.5) and that He called the Pharisees 'fools and blind' (Matt. 23.17). He told His disciples to give to everyone that asked (6.30) but the wise virgins are commended for refusing to give away their oil (Matt. 25.8-9). It is at least clear that literalism is out of place.

'Lay not up treasure upon earth' (Matt. 6.19) He said. If this is to be taken literally as a warning against thrift, most of us could easily reach perfection. What could be easier than not saving money? If however our Lord is really calling for detachment of spirit from the love of money, then it is a hard saying. But it is idle to quote it if extravagant living makes us a burden upon others, or makes it impossible for us to provide for our families. The fact that we have not taken thought for the morrow does not make our carelessness Christian.

St. Augustine said that the rule of Jesus was 'Love God and do what you like'. That saying goes to the root of it, because in so far as we do love God truly we shall do as He wills and we shall like to do it. Jesus commended the insight of the lawyer who summed up the law in love for God and one's neighbour: 'Thou shalt love the Lord thy God with all thy heart and with all thy soul and with all thy strength and with all thy mind; and thy neighbour as thyself' (10.25-28. The reply was a combination of Deut. 6.5 with Lev. 19.18). So St. Paul dared to say that when a Jew became a Christian the Mosaic Law and its commandments were no longer binding. 'If ye are led by the Spirit ye are not under the law' (Gal. 5.18). 'For the whole law is fulfilled in one word, Thou shalt love thy neighbour as thyself' (Gal. 5.14; cf. Rom. 13.8-10).

What Jesus gives us is not a new set of commandments but rather illustrations of how love acts in certain circumstances, as for example in the story of the Good Samaritan which He told the lawyer instead of a definition of the word 'neighbour'. In other circumstances love might behave otherwise. What, for example, should the Good Samaritan have done if he had arrived half an hour earlier and found the robbers in the act of attacking the traveller? Through watching Jesus in the circumstances of His land and time, dealing with men and women and their problems, through studying His teaching, and through opening our hearts and minds to His living Spirit we can come to know 'the mind of Christ' (1 Cor. 2.16) and in the light of it to face the different problems of our own generation.

3

The motive which He constantly urged upon men was that they should behave worthily of their Father, as true sons: ' Love your enemies and do them good, and lend, never despairing; and your reward shall be great, and ye shall be sons of the Most High; for He is kind toward the unthankful and evil. Be ye merciful even as your Father is merciful ' (6.35-36). Goodness is God likeness, or in an old-fashioned but most Christian word, godliness.

It is with the inward motive that Jesus is most concerned. He traces the act back to the thought and feeling from which it springs, to the will and the disposition. The same act done from different motives and in a different spirit would have different moral worth in His eyes (21.1-4; 18.9-14). It is because His requirement is inward that the sayings search our souls as they do. We congratulate ourselves on our self-control, on not breaking out into angry speech or action. So far, so good, but what, asks Jesus, about your thoughts? The angry thought is wrong too. Keep yourself not only from adultery but even from the lustful look.

What should we spontaneously do if we were set free from all inhibitions and restraints? It sounds harsh when Jesus declares that men will be judged by their idle words, rather than by their deliberate ones (Matt. 12.36). But his idle words, what he says when he is off his guard, are the clue to a man's character. ' The good man out of the good treasure of his heart bringeth forth that which is good; and the evil man out of the evil treasure bringeth forth that which is evil: for out of the abundance of the heart his mouth speaketh ' (6.45).

That is why Jesus thought it a greater thing to be able to say ' Forgiven ' to the paralysed man than to say ' Walk '. The root of the trouble was in the man's heart, his ' unconscious ' in modern jargon—the results of sins and memories of the past and fears for the future. Forgiveness went down to the real source, and by removing the obstacle opened the way to the healing of the whole man, body and soul (5.17-26).

4

If we loved God and men truly we should need no rules

and rules would be of little help. It is impossible to decide
how a Christian ought to behave in a particular situation by
consulting a concordance and looking up the texts. Each
hour brings its own unforeseeable challenge and the Christian meets it guided by the word spoken to him then by
the Spirit of Christ. Guidance comes in real life situations
rather than in codes of rules. Christians can never claim
infallibility. We fail in our knowledge of God, of the facts
of the case, and of the ' neighbour ' who at the moment con-
fronts us. We fail because our readiness to do the will of
God is incomplete and because we are crippled by past
faithlessness. But every Christian knows that the guidance
and empowering of God are realities, always available if
we will accept them.

It is, of course, an absolute and impossible standard that
Jesus holds before us. No man loves God with all his heart
and soul and strength and mind. No man can be perfect
as his heavenly Father is perfect (Matt. 5.48). That is an
old and familiar ground of attack on the Christian Faith.
' I well know,' said Trypho, the Jewish opponent of Justin
Martyr, ' that your Christian precepts out of what is called
the Gospel are great and admirable, so admirable indeed
that I doubt if any one can keep them.' This would be a
valid criticism if these were rules to be observed as a condition of church membership. Christ's call to His followers
is to surrender to the love of God, and in the measure in
which they do, then by the aid of the Holy Spirit there will
be born and will grow in their hearts the desire to embody
in their own lives the likeness of His. They will never
attain, and the more complete their consecration the more
they will be aware of their failure. The ethics of Jesus
contain both a challenge and a gift, and the possibility of a
growing approximation to an impossible and therefore
worthwhile ideal. Happily for us the fundamental Christian message concerns not what we ought to do, but what
God has done and what God is willing to do. In fellowship
with Him and with others who are likewise trying to be like
Him we can be lifted above our own native possibilities.

' Brethren,' wrote St. Paul, ' I count not myself yet to have
apprehended : but one thing I do, forgetting the things which
are behind, and stretching forward to the things which are
before, I press on toward the goal unto the prize of the high

(margin, *upward*) calling of God in Christ Jesus ' (Phil. 3.13-14).

It was not the craving for paradox but deep insight that led Whitehead to speak of ' mankind's most precious instrument of progress—the impracticable ethics of Christianity '.

5

Jesus constantly emphasized in particular two implications of His way of life, forgiveness and service.

Jesus does not call us only to natural human kindliness. It is easy enough to be good to those who are good to us (6.32,33). The test comes when we have been badly treated, when anger calls for retaliation. There is nothing more emphatic or more characteristic in the teaching of Jesus than His urging of the necessity of forgiveness. Nothing so poisons the soul as to cherish hatred. Nothing so shuts the door against God. We can only receive the forgiveness of God if we extend forgiveness to our fellows (11.3-4; 17.3-4; cf. Matt. 6.14-15). And could there be a more moving demonstration of the teaching by the teacher than those words from the Cross: ' Father, forgive them, for they know not what they do ' (23.34). Here as ever goodness is God likeness (6.35-36).

The way of Jesus is also supremely the way of service. This too has inevitably been emphasized at many points in our study. He condemned an order of society in which ' the haves ' exploit ' the have nots '. The mark of greatness in His Kingdom is service. ' The kings of the Gentiles have lordship over them; and they that have authority over them are called Benefactors. But ye shall not be so: but he that is the greater among you let him become as the younger; and he that is chief as he that doth serve. . . . I am in the midst of you as he that serveth ' (22.25-27). So also the life of greed and acquisitiveness in which a man is dominated by the motive of personal gain instead of service is impossible for His followers: ' Ye cannot serve God and Mammon ' (16.13-15).

Of that way of service Jesus gave many examples in His own life. They are too many to enumerate here, and there is no need. His teaching also contains many illustrations of what He meant. The Good Samaritan sums up unforgettably the duty of care for the needy and unfortunate. The same spirit of Christian love seeking to do 'likewise' has found tasks in every generation: abolishing slavery as well as helping the slave; preventing disease as well as caring for the sick; seeking a social order without poverty and not only giving alms to the poor. If Jesus did give us a rule at all it was 'the golden rule': 'As ye would that men should do to you, do ye also to them likewise' (6.31).

6

Christianity, it must be said again, is a Gospel and not a burden: good news of a gift rather than a demand. When Jesus described the citizens of His Kingdom in the Beatitudes He called them 'blessed' or 'happy': 'the people to be congratulated' is a phrase that conveys something of the idea. The doing of God's will may call for renunciation and persecution and poverty—even for death. But it always brings great reward (6.20-35). This is not to say that Jesus told men to be good because they would be rewarded. People who do that certainly get a reward of a kind, but it is not the one Jesus meant (Matt. 6.2-5). He explicitly warned His followers against such selfish 'goodness' (6.32-34).

There is a great difference between seeking the approval of God and working for a reward from man. For in the sight of God it is useless to bestow all our goods to feed the poor, if we have not love (1 Cor. 13.3). God knows the heart. Insincerity and self-seeking here defeats its own end.

It is indeed rather a result than a reward that the richest gifts life can offer here or hereafter come to the unselfish and self-forgetful. If goodness is God likeness, then goodness must of necessity lead men further into the knowledge and blessedness of God. We cannot *earn* God's favour: we receive His good gifts. The motive is not the reward but grateful love.

Certainly Jesus did not promise earthly prosperity to His disciples. That is an unfounded and dangerous notion that keeps on raising its head in spite of His clear teaching. Rather He promised to some poverty and persecution, and many of the noblest of Christians have received them. Yet the Christian life is life indeed (9.24; 17.33; cf. John 10.10) whether in this world or the next. 'Blessed are ye' (6.20-23). 'Rejoice that your names are written in heaven' (10.20).

And the real Christians, the ordinary everyday ones, or those enduring suffering or persecution, or the martyrs, do in fact rejoice.

Renan said that Luke's Gospel was 'a book full of joy'. It is. Is it surprising with such a story to tell that an irresistible joy rings through its pages? It opens and closes with thanksgiving. It ends with the risen Jesus triumphant over death, foretelling the spread of the Faith among all nations and promising 'power from on high'. 'And they worshipped him, and returned to Jerusalem with great joy; and were continually in the temple blessing God' (24.52-53).

The last word of the Gospel is joy.

SUBJECT INDEX

INDEX OF BIBLICAL REFERENCES

*(The figures printed in italics refer to
page numbers in the book)*